D1624424

THE SECRET TO LIFE TRANSFORMATION

HOW TO CLAIM YOUR DESTINY NOW!

JULIE CHRYSTYN

ISBN-10: 1-59777-581-9
ISBN-13: 978-1-59777-581-6
Library of Congress Cataloging-In-Publication Data Available

Book Design by Sonia Fiore

Printed in the United States of America

Dove Books, Inc.
9465 Wilshire Boulevard, Suite 840
Beverly Hills, CA 90212

10 9 8 7 6 5 4 3 2 1

To

DWIGHT D. OPPERMAN

FOREWORD BY LARRY KING

I HAD ABOUT AS much of a chance of becoming a media icon as did a dirt-poor kid from the former Communist Yugoslavia of landing on the Forbes list. But the believers among us pursue our dreams against all odds, create visions far beyond our realities, and go for the gold in defiance of obstacles.

Regardless of appearances, there was nothing ignorant or blissful about our journey—a journey that had more twists and turns than the road from Maui to Hana, but one that took us both to the heights of our desired destinations.

At last, I confess all in my new autobiography, *What Am I Doing Here?* On the other hand, Julie Chrystyn penned an inspiring and motivating guide, *The Secret to Life Transformation*, which spills the secrets of how the likes of me get to be King. By the time you get to the last page, no stone will be left unturned when it comes to empowering *you* to change your life from what it is to what you want it to be—regardless of your circumstances and environment.

Is it hype or reality? It's a home run! For nearly two decades as a ghostwriter, Julie was the invisible wordsmith behind those compelling "autobiographies" of some of the most famous and infamous political and business leaders across the globe. She became a successful businessperson in her own right and is now a noted philanthropist.

For years, her publisher has been telling me that she's the only person he knows who can utter a thought and the next thing you know, it has come to fruition. Julie Chrystyn has lived every word she preaches. She has interviewed hundreds of others who have done the same and now shares their secrets of success with you. She pursued her lifelong quest of distinguishing the difference between the "haves" and "have-nots." The result is not only a truly magical life transformation of her own but also this exceptional and extraordinary book, which will take you on your own path to greater success and happiness.

Larry King

INTRODUCTION

There is a statement in the Bible that has never left my consciousness. After the Israelites were led out of Egypt to the Promised Land, God finally spoke: "Why has it taken you forty years to make an eleven-day journey?" That's right, the Chosen spent four decades going around and around and around the mountain when they could have arrived in the land of milk and honey in a mere week and a half!

How many of us have spent years, even decades, in pursuit of our hopes, goals, and desired destinations only to discover that we're back where we started, or lagging even further behind? How many wrong turns, U-turns, and long journeys have we taken only to meet setback, heartbreak, and a loss of the will to go on? How often have we done the same thing over and over again, while expecting different results? How many of us have given passion and support to those offering change for our nation but have not made any serious change in our own lives?

There is only one source that can transform your life from what it is to what you want it to be—and that is you. So few individuals possess the owner's manual of success by instinct. As one who was born into an oppressive communist regime and lived life full-circle, I have had a lifelong obsession with trying to comprehend why so few people truly prosper, while the majority merely survive. We have been served up everything from "the secret" to great philosophical and theoretical explanations, but the only wisdom that matters on the subject, at the end of the day, is the one offered up by those who have actually created something out of seemingly nothing.

Toward that end, I have interviewed and corresponded with more than 300 ordinary people who have accomplished, by anyone's account, the most extraordinary things. I spent three years in more than a dozen countries and repeatedly visited numerous states while on my quest. In fact, last year I spent a total of seven weeks at home. The result equipped me with a mind-boggling arsenal of knowledge and wisdom about what it truly means to be a self-made person. The hardest thing was narrowing the list to just twelve individuals from completely diverse walks of life who best exemplify the lesson that needs to be driven home. We are limited by space, not by a shortage of worthy examples.

King Solomon was the wealthiest man who ever lived, even by today's standards. He had a mantra: "Without a vision, the people perish." Without a vision there can be no success, no life. Do you have a dream? *The Secret to Life Transformation* will show you how to turn your dream into your vision, and your vision into your reality. Now.

Julie Chrystyn
Bel Air, California
November 18, 2008

“We do not merely observe and interpret reality; we *create* it.”

THE POWER OF A TRANSFORMED MIND

NOTHING GIVES US MORE pleasure than accomplishing something previously deemed impossible. The spirit to achieve lives within us, drives us to heights and distances beyond what we can see, hear, and touch. We know that there is more to life than what we perceive with our senses. We are uncomfortable and unsatisfied when we feel disconnected from the realm of the supernatural.

Poor education and trips around the mountain for years or decades have left too many people without hope or purpose. However, an age is slowly but surely dawning when people's desires are meeting their destinies, and they are manifesting them into reality in great numbers. Such has always been the master plan. In Genesis 1:28, God instructs us to "Be fruitful and multiply; fill the earth and subdue it; have dominion over the fish of the sea, over the birds of the air, and over every living thing that moves on the earth."

According to *Webster's*, to have dominion means to rule or have the power to rule; to have sovereignty and sovereign authority. In legal terms it means having ownership. Now, dominion over every living thing that moves on the earth—that's quite a gift and responsibility! And it does not say "some of you," or "a select few," or "the chosen ones," but every single individual that God has created. Yes, *you* have dominion over every living thing on earth.

In 1900 the philosopher and author William James wrote: "The human individual…lives usually far within his limits; he possesses powers of various sorts which he habitually fails to use." James examined our "habit of inferiority" and stated that we operate under subconscious, self-imposed limitations and never even come to this awareness. Others have built on his insight, labeling the many ways in which we restrict ourselves as "repression."

We view the world through the vision of our own thoughts and beliefs. Thus, there may be a vast distance between what is real and what we perceive to be real. At the end of the day, the fundamental truth is mind-boggling. Simply stated, we do not merely observe and interpret reality; we *create* it. You've heard the expression, "You are what you eat." Well, in reality, you are what you *think*. Depending on your state of mind, this is either welcome news or an absolute bomb. However, you start to create the life you really want only when you comprehend the nature of reality and begin to consciously direct your thoughts. Realizing that you live in a vast, infinite universe of energy will become the turning point in your life.

It was certainly the turning point in mine. As an immigrant child struggling at every conceivable level in a new and strange world, with parents whose primary struggle was to put a roof over our heads, food on the table, and to provide a decent education for my brother and me, worry became the constant drumming backbeat of my life. My father taught me to believe that if I didn't struggle and sacrifice, our very survival would be at stake. I considered worry a way of life, and if for a moment I didn't worry, I worried that I wasn't worrying and felt like a sluggard! Needless to say, this led to a lot of anxiety, illness, and a lack of prosperity and happiness. I don't fault my parents. I never did. They did the best they could. I always knew that they had my best interests at heart, but eventually the burden became so enormous that I had to learn the truth and create a very different reality for myself. This was no overnight accomplishment. But if my father were alive today to see just how far I've come, the shock of it would probably kill him.

So many people fall prey to the lie that life is just what we have now, that it will always be predictably this way. Whatever problems and issues you are focusing on right now will be your problems and issues tomorrow; you are perpetuating them into your future. You assure your lack of financial security in the future by worrying about the lack of it right now. You guarantee your lack of future success by thinking about all the obstacles that will keep you from getting there. You are aging faster because you are quite aware of how a modern, stress-filled life is causing you to age prematurely. Examine your thoughts and review the life you have created. If you say to yourself, "I can't do that," you won't. On the other hand, if you assert to yourself that what you want is possible, that what you want is attainable, and that what you want is something you deserve, it's a just a matter of time until you find the means to achieve it.

Success is energy. Fame is energy. Love is energy. Failure is energy. Illness is energy. Gucci shoes and a brand-new BMW are energy. So is your beat-up Toyota. A lack of motivation and excitement about your life is energy, as is the thrill of knowing that what you are about to do will rock the world! I often witness this in a magical seven-year-old girl I know. If you told her that we were going to visit a concentration camp, she would say, "Oh, boy! Let's go to camp!"

What is out there is determined by what is within us. This theory was demonstrated by the great Nobel laureate and scientist Werner Karl Heisenberg, who discovered one of the central principles of modern physics. It was named after him: the

Heisenberg Uncertainty Principle. Heisenberg demonstrated that on a subatomic level, the observer, by the decisions he made, affected the outcome of a physics experiment. This was the first time that the scientific community recognized that the observer and the act of observing were inseparable from what was observed. In lay terms, you can perceive events in your life as you wish, but what you choose to perceive will change the energy of that situation or circumstance, and thus change the reality.

Is science beginning to prove what the Bible has said all along? Mark 11:24 states, "Therefore I say unto you, what things soever you desire, when you pray, believe that you receive them, and you shall have them." It doesn't say "some of the things you desire." It doesn't say "three of the things you desire." It doesn't say "depending on when and what you desire," but "what soever you desire." If you believe, you shall have it.

I recently ran across a bit of fascinating information. In 1993, a scientifically validated study was undertaken in Washington, D.C., to determine if deliberate and concentrated meditation could have any effect on the city's crime rate. Even the greatest optimists were floored by the results. During the weeks that just a few volunteers meditated, the crime rate fell by an astounding twenty-five percent.

Is meditation a form of prayer? How worthwhile is prayer? James 5:16–18 explains: "The prayer of a righteous man is powerful and effective. Elijah was a man just like us. He prayed earnestly that it would not rain, and it did not rain on the land for three and a half years. Again he prayed, and the heavens gave rain, and the earth produced its crops."

Jesus taught, "I tell you the truth, if you have faith as small as a mustard seed, you can say to this mountain, 'Move from here to there,' and it will move. Nothing will be impossible for you" (Matthew 17:20). We are further told in 2 Corinthians 10:4–5: "The weapons we fight with are not the weapons of the world. On the contrary, they have divine power to demolish strongholds. We demolish arguments and every pretension that sets itself up against the knowledge of God, and we take captive every thought to make it obedient to Christ." Ephesians 6:18 declares, "Pray in the Spirit of all occasions with all kinds of prayers and requests. With this in mind, be alert and always keep on praying for all the saints [people]."

The person praying, the passion behind the prayer, or the purpose of the prayer does not matter. The laws of the universe apply to all of us at all times and in all ways. If you don't believe in the law of gravity, you will still fall if you step off the ledge.

So how should we engage in prayer? There are no right or wrong ways. It is not something that you need to be taught in order to get the desired results. No eloquence or wordiness is required in order to have your intentions known. In fact, Jesus warned against repetitiousness and rebuked those who were not sincere in their prayers. "And when you pray, do not keep on babbling like pagans," He said in Mark 6:7–8, "for they think they will be heard because of their many words. Do not be like them, for your Father knows what you need before you ask him." Such power of prayer was well demonstrated in Psalm 107:28–30: "Then they cried out to the Lord in their trouble, and He brought them out of their distress. He stilled the storm to a whisper; the waves of the seas were hushed. They were glad when it grew calm, and He guided them to their desired haven."

The power of prayer has overcome enemies (Psalm 6:9–10), conquered death (2 Kings 4:3–36), brought healing (James 5:14–15), and defeated demons (Mark 9:29). Through prayer, eyes are opened, hearts are changed, wounds are healed, and wisdom is granted.

What is your desired haven? How do you turn your dreams into reality? Start by understanding that your thoughts are the creators of all things. You alone are responsible for the energy you pull in. When you are the source of positive thought energy, the same will return to you. Likewise, negative energy will attract its own kind.

It is vital to realize that nothing stands still. It never did and it never will. While virtually all matter appears motionless to the naked eye, in reality there is no solid matter whatsoever. The hardest piece of steel is just a well-orchestrated mass of revolving particles. As we know, the unseen atom is nature's building block, from which come trees, stones, my cat, and Christian Louboutin stilettos.

All matter is in a constant state of vibration—it literally moves nonstop. The molecule consists of fast-moving particles we call atoms, and the atoms are made up of fast-moving protons, neutrons, and electrons. Within every single particle of matter lies an unseen force that makes the atoms circle around each other at an unimaginable speed. A single rate of vibration produces sound. Our ears can only detect the sound that comes from twenty to twenty thousand cycles per second. As the cycles increase, they are manifested as heat. Further up the scale, vibrations or cycles register in the form of light. This includes the invisible ultraviolet rays and energy with a wavelength of an even higher order—it cannot be seen, but it sure can be felt!

Progressing up the scale, the vibrations create the power, many progressive-thinking individuals believe, with which people *think*. Whether you subscribe to biblical teachings or science—it is certain that *thoughts are energy*. To take a lesson from chemistry in this instance, we may conclude that the only differences between thought, sound, heat, and light are the number of vibrations per second. It also means that thought travels, imparts energy, and has consequences.

Perhaps Alexander Graham Bell posed the question best: "If the thought waves are similar to the wireless waves, they must pass from the brain and flow endlessly around the world and the universe. The body and the skull and other solid substances would form no obstruction to their passage, as they pass through the ether that surrounds the molecules of every substance, no matter how solid or dense. Thus, you ask if there would not be constant interference and confusion if other people's thoughts were flowing through our brains and setting up thoughts in them that did not originate within ourselves?"

Many of us claim to be independent thinkers, but how often is that truly the case? In the course of any given day we are usually bombarded with negative thoughts, scenarios, and energies. Some originate within us, but many are absorbed from external sources. Friends, professional associations, casual encounters, the media in all its forms—they are all informing us of what is happening in the world, or they are entertaining us in such a way as to redirect our thoughts and alter the course of our intended thinking. They influence us by telling us what is worthy and what is not, who is hot and who is not, what is the best medical care, food to eat, clothing to wear, car to drive, and deodorant to use. Add to these the office phone, e-mail, cell phone, and text messages, and all become woven into reality. These thoughts are the metaphorical electrical currents that cannot be seen, but whose effects can certainly be felt.

All the external influences that we internalize cause us to become who we are. How much of a conscious hand have you had in creating who you are today? How many of us invest the time to raise our own consciousness enough to practice discernment, to distinguish what is required for success and happiness from what are merely effects of the outside influences, manipulations, and persuasions that engulf us? At stake may be your money, your vote, your action, or even your passivity as part of a desired mass consciousness designed to keep you low, quiet, and out of the way. Once you become a programmed worker ant or are locked into a predetermined mind-set, it becomes very challenging indeed to be self-sufficiently content and prosperous.

Of course, as you become more of an individual and more in command of your own thinking and actions, more people will direct their thoughts and their energies toward you.

This is what Bell was talking about. The pendulum can swing in any direction—some people will admire you, some will be jealous or slanderous, some will hate you and plot against you, and some will love you and open doors for you. If you are a doctor, people will place a certain burden on you. If you are a politician, you will get the blame for all the ills of our nation. In any event, the ability to nurture your own sense of self and determine your own course of action will be tested. It is not enough to transform your mind and your actions. It is necessary to reaffirm this transformation at every turn. It is easy to be derailed, but the true test of consciousness, of awareness, and of your truly transformed self is how well you absorb these attempts at derailment and continue to assert your needs, your thoughts, and all the things you deserve.

“Life must be confronted without flinching.”

"AN UNTHINKABLE JOURNEY" —JUSTICE CLARENCE THOMAS

It wasn't an epiphany at any point, but rather over time I saw a contrast. My grandfather taught me something that I could only appreciate over time. He taught me that there was a direct connection between having the simple things in life, like a toilet that flushes, and hard work. He would say over and over again, "You have three choices: You could steal to get something, you could inherit, or you could work for it." The first two were not options. So you had one choice. If you wanted a different life, you had to work, and he was going to teach us how to work. It wasn't the road to Damascus. It unfolded over time.

My journey is unthinkable in any other country. If I had been born in a culture that did not prize merit, if I had been born into a culture that was controlled by caste systems, then I would never have been able to go from Pinpoint, Georgia, to the Supreme Court. If I had been born in a country that did not undergo the wrenching changes of America in the last half of the twentieth century, then my story would not have been one of triumph over adversity, but mute suffering leading to an unremarkable death. I have seen that happen to people, many people, over the course of my life.

The integration of American society that began in my youth has proceeded rapidly to undoing the barriers that had traditionally stood against advancement—for African-Americans as well as the poor. But it was not integration-by-law that allowed me to advance. It was not something imposed from without that drove me to succeed. It was the values, the discipline, and the hard work that I learned from my grandfather that gave me the chance to excel when the opportunities for advancement presented themselves. It's all very well to believe, as some do, that the historical experience of being black is sufficient to entitle you to preferential treatment, but the truth of the matter is that if you can't do the work, then you don't deserve the job. I learned this at my grandfather's knee (and at the end of his strap) from my earliest days in his home. I was driven to succeed not because the government came along one day and said that I could, but because my grandfather had sacrificed and worked hard his whole life to give me the chances that he never had. To honor his effort, I felt that I had to achieve a success that had been denied him, as well as so many others, by the evils of segregation in the Jim Crow South. Civil rights legislation was all very well, but without hard work and self-reliance it would not have been enough.

The values I learned from my grandfather helped me from the time I met my first challenge, and they have helped me ever since. It was his unwillingness to bend in the face of adversity that made his effort count, I came to realize. His unwillingness to make (or accept) any excuses for any setback whatsoever made his an unwavering example of the way that life must be confronted: without flinching. The right set of character traits, the right set of habits of hard work, the right set of beliefs, the right set of discipline about living your life and conducting your affairs—these were the things that my grandparents believed would serve me throughout my life. And they have.

The same was true with the nuns who educated us. I used to leave a little saying on my desk: "Luck is where preparation and opportunity meet." You really don't have much control over opportunity. You might have a little bit, insofar as you can change your circumstances. But what you do have control over is preparing yourself so that when the opportunity comes, you're ready. As Lincoln said, "I will prepare myself and when the time comes, I will be ready." Some people I met during youth said, "Why are you even trying? It looks impossible!" Literally, it's because of faith. Where does the faith come from? It came from everybody around me growing up. I had a set of people around me who, despite the circumstances, never despaired. They never gave up.

They were religious—they believed in God. We had a society in which even people who didn't regularly go to church had faith. I can't speak for others, but that appears to have diminished. Still, even those who don't believe in God or run away from organized religion continue to reach out, asking the same questions as people have asked all over the world: "Isn't there more?" There is something that drives people to seek answers and look beyond their immediate circumstances for them. There are tragedies and setbacks that people have in their lives that cause them to look past homilies in search of deeper answers. This always takes me back to the old spirituals. The people who sang them in the prewar South and in the years and generations of Jim Crow—their circumstances were so dire that they knew there simply had to be more. And those people weren't well educated, so they looked at it and said, "There's something transcended." It was an article of their faith that they knew that the next world had to be better than this one. This is an essential part of the legacy I inherited from my circumstances, my grandparents, and the generations of toil and endurance that I came from.

I started as an altar boy, went through the seminary, and was going to be a priest…so religion was an integral and formal part of my life. I was educated by nuns, Irish nuns, and went to Catholic schools until I got out of college. So faith was always front and center. It was a routine part of my education, a part of my life. And when you're a kid, you kind of go through the motions. But when you become an adult, and times get difficult, and you look around you and there are no obvious answers in front of you—where do you go? You go back to the transcendent set of principles that you learned when you were a kid, that have been a part of your life through your youth, your development, that have never gone away. It's part of a seamless blanket that forms your life. So I would say it was always there. You rely on it to survive those circumstances and you rely on it as a guide to provide you with "faith, hope, and charity," as we always said. And hope—it gave you hope, it gave you the sense that there was a reason to get up every day even when it didn't look like there was an end point, a light at the end of the tunnel. You had to have hope that there would be. The ultimate giving up is when there is no more hope.

Where does hope come from? When you don't have money and you don't know how you're going to pay for anything and you don't know how you're going to make it through the day—where do you get your hope? If you're sick, if you're hurt, where do you go? In my case, the powerful model of my grandparents was always borne home to me. They literally put their lives on the altar and became human sacrifices so that my brother and I could have a chance. They always said, "We're going to make it possible for you to have a chance that we never had." That informs and animates everything I do, everything. Because I could never accept that their sacrifice was in vain. Their hope in the face of circumstances that would have crippled others, their perseverance in the face of prejudice, segregation, and hostility has been the constant beacon of my life. Without their example, without being able to draw on their experience, then I would have been a bitter drifter, unwilling to accept the possibility that life offered more. Without their example of hard work in the face of terrible deprivation—and with no relief in sight—then my own resolution in the face of my difficulties may well have wavered many times.

They believed that if you worked hard there would be some reward—like crops in the field. But the more life experience you gain, the more you can see that there are not always fair outcomes, that in spite of hard work and good values, there are plenty of people who do not get rewarded, and are even forced to suffer more. In my youth, this contradiction caused me to act out my anger at times. As I began to see the bigger picture, that there were injustices that never got righted and innocent people who were punished unjustly, I began to feel the anger that consumed so many of my peers. When I was going to college in the late 1960s and 1970s, there were riots in the cities—I saw them and I was moved by the struggles of those times. I participated in protests and I did embody some of the anger of those times.

It was only as I grew and matured and reflected on the causes of that collective anger that I began to see a larger picture. The theories of people who declared themselves "experts"—especially on race relations—were not really designed to address the real problems of the community as I had experienced them, but simply to assuage a lot of white guilt. I began to see this political condescension from the time I graduated from Yale Law School. It seemed that everywhere I turned, people were trying to deal with "the black problem." But their programs did not emphasize the values that had allowed me to succeed. On the contrary, self-reliance, hard work, and discipline were exactly the qualities that were downgraded by affirmative action, busing, and the other measures the federal government had imposed. I felt for many years that people were not really seeing the same problems that I was seeing, and though for a time this fed into my anger, I realized that in fact there was a way to think about these issues reasonably and realistically, if not in a way that was politically popular.

The values my grandparents had taught me may not have been popular, but they had been effective. How could it be that they could not even be considered feasible by people who were busy assuring us of the purity of their intentions? How could my grandparents have been so politically wrong? Well, after careful reflection, I came up with a simple answer: they weren't. And any system, any politician, any theory that tried to say that they were? They were the ones who were wrong. My faith in my grandparents helped sustain my faith in myself and the values that they taught me.

There is a line in a wonderful song by Esther Satterfield, "The Need to Be," that says, "I cannot be the reflection of a man." My goodness, there it was! I can't be the reflection of other peoples' conduct. I can't be the reflection of your anger, can't be the reflection of what you've done to me. In other words, people cannot define themselves by their angry reactions to what others might think of them. You have to have your own integrity. That was the integrity that I always sought. In order to do that, you have to unfetter yourself from all the things that may have happened to you that you considered unfair, from your own natural reactions to injustices you may have suffered. You must free yourself from these things and not let them affect how you conduct your life.

The litany of humility has been invaluable to me. Learning to distinguish between those things I can change and those that I can't has been a constant source of renewal. Focusing on my own ability to effect change has made it possible for me to change myself. It has made it possible for me to transcend dire circumstances in my youth, anger in my young adulthood, and bruising politics in my adulthood. By concentrating on my work, by putting into effect the values that were instilled in me—that is how I have managed to transcend and transform my circumstances. This is a lesson I have tried to impart. Despite the fact that it is impossible to always know if your lesson is being understood or properly applied, it is faith in the message that keeps you going.

You try to bring others along. You try. You can throw seed on good ground or bad ground. All you try to do is treat others the way you want to be treated. To treat them with dignity, respect, fairness—even if they don't treat you that way. And you will be amazed. The seed may take; it may not take. It may take a while! But I've been going across this country now in different capacities for almost thirty years. You will always have a feud. You have the cynics and the media. You have the skeptics, the people who are always negative. But at the core, you have a lot of good people.

Native American ladies cleaning tables at a Salt Lake City function last year surrounded me like I was a long-lost brother. I hadn't been there in a decade. Yet there they were, thanking me and telling me how much they admired me. What is it? I didn't know these ladies. But they sensed that, in a profound way, we were connected. And once they sensed that I was one of them, their pride and affection moved them to embrace me. So you can affect people that way. I have found nuggets of people who will suddenly say, "Because you tried to be good, because you try to do the right thing, I'm going to try." These moments are priceless, and countless. Cynics may sneer at the human spirit. But I have seen it in action and it does more than move mountains; it changes what many believe immutable.

It's tougher today than it was before, because we had a culture that enforced or was permeated with the notion that there is a transcendent being, that there's a reason to hope, there's a reason to have faith. Now we have a society that talks about how "we are the source." That's nihilism and that's something politicians have taken advantage of to further their own careers. Government cannot solve all problems, though there is no shortage of people who seem to believe that it can. And if it cannot, then there are experts who claim to be able to. But if they don't do it, then we say, "It's not going to happen." This environment makes the kind of transcendent hope I've been talking about seem impossible, and in the current environment it certainly seems more difficult. But the message of hope is its own justification. Through hope and faith it has been shown that even the direst circumstances can be overcome, even the most brutal poverty can flourish into prosperity, and even the most abject of cynics can be restored to belief.

I used to pass this little church years ago in northern Virginia, just a tiny little church—I think it was a black church. And it always had that sign out front, "For we walk by faith, not by sight." Rarely has such a profound truth been put so neatly.

“Leaders are people who are perceived to be free from the influences that occupy the rest of us most of the time.”

YOU—THE INDEPENDENT THINKER

WHAT DOES IT TAKE to be a leader and not a follower? How does a person become independent, in their thoughts and in their actions, when so much of life seems to be about following? Consider all the things you are asked to follow: news, technology, trends, celebrities, the stock market, and your favorite sports teams. This list is partial, of course, but it represents a huge amount of information and interest in just a few of the human endeavors people are involved in. It is easy to get bogged down in any one of these things to the exclusion of all else, and many people do.

If you do pay attention to the news, which news? Print, TV, magazines, the Internet? Right-wing, left-wing, a combination for balance? Do you follow individual stories or just go for an overview? Which overview? And that's just for starters. What about technology? Do you have TiVo? Bluetooth? DVR? Satellite television? A BlackBerry? And what kind of computer do you use? Okay, that may be too much already…but wait, there's more. If you follow fashion, what kind? Haute couture? Retro? *Vogue*, *GQ*? Getting a little tired? How about just a little light celebrity-gazing? *Entertainment Tonight*? *TMZ*?

The National Enquirer? *People*? *Us Weekly*? Paris Hilton? Okay, okay, this is getting long but…nowhere near complete. What about sports? Dozens of channels are devoted to nothing else. ESPN? *Sports Illustrated*? Just scores and results? Football, baseball, basketball (men's and women's), hockey, soccer… again, a partial list. Let's not even think about the amounts of information on the stock market, because your head could explode.

Think about the things that get left out: your friends, your spouse, and your family, whom you are expected to keep up with if you have the time after you've been flooded with the overwhelming amount of things that are "normal." To be a leader and not a follower today, it is necessary to cultivate your own garden, often at the expense of something or someone very important to you. Why is this so? Why does it seem to be a zero-sum game, where the cultivation of one interest must come at the expense of another? Is there no other way to be a leader?

To be a leader requires one thing: independent thinking. Leaders are not the people who seize the flag and go charging into battle screaming at the top of their lungs for everyone else to "Follow me!" Not anymore. Leaders are people who are perceived to be free from the influences that occupy the rest of us most of the time. They have the perception and the calm to keep their heads, especially when everyone else is shouting at the top of their lungs. They retain their own self-interest as well as perceive the interests of others in a balanced way. How do they do it? What allows someone to remain uncluttered, clear-eyed, and sharp? It starts with the way that person thinks.

Independent thinkers understand that the media, in all their outlets, are a business. As a business they cannot survive without your attention. It's the Great Dane in your house, on your streets and highways, and in your office. Well, maybe "Great Dane" understates the problem. Come to think of it, so does "800-pound gorilla." It has become more like the 8,000-pound gorilla that has grown so enormous, it's impossible *not* to talk about, but still…nothing can be done about its size. The constant blare of the media in every American's life has become a fact of nature. Once this is accepted, the media are reduced to their proper size—significant, interesting, but not definitive. The media alone cannot change your life. You have to be willing to let them, first. An independent thinker understands the media's role, accepts their function…and moves on.

It's easy to be overwhelmed by the sheer staggering weight of all the information you are expected to assimilate on any given day. But the ability to filter out the more useless and time-wasting elements of the media barrage is a priority for anyone who wants to stop following the herd and start leading it. The scale of the assault is huge, so you must make equally enormous efforts to protect yourself from it. A clear insight into what is most important to you is the key. What matters? Are new media outlets designed with you in mind really giving you the information you need? Is it really necessary for you to spend hours every day just passively soaking it up? Do the things you learn in this way really enhance your life? These questions are not casual. They are usually just below the surface of any consumer's awareness, and for good reason. If we honestly asked ourselves what would happen if we just turned it all off one day, we might find a disturbing answer: not much harm would follow, and perhaps a lot of good. Just for starters, then, try turning everything off for twenty-four hours. Afterward, ask yourself, just what was it that you missed?

There are other impediments to being an independent thinker. People in your life may play very important roles—your spouse, your boss, your kids—but are you interacting with them in ways that are meaningful? Do you feel the love and support from your spouse that should renew you every day? Or is your spouse caught up in the frenzy, too? Do you get the guidance and motivation from your boss that you should, or are you just reacting to the crisis of the day? Are you able to give your kids the kind of time and attention that will teach them the values and the love that you want to give them? Or are you just too busy? Certainly there are compromises that everyone must make with the demands of life, but some sacrifices come at too high a price. Would you rather have your kids brought up by the media, which have endless amounts of time and resources to capture their attention? Or do you want them to have core beliefs, real values, and respect for their elders, their society, and themselves?

Independent thinking is not just a requirement for being a leader; it is absolutely necessary for anyone who hopes to have control over his or her life. It is easy to see how people let themselves be swayed by the media. The demands of the modern world are such as to require a two-parent, two-income family to work a great deal of the time. After work they are expected to have quality family time as well. And to keep up with the latest news, trends, and so forth. If you don't make a clear plan for dealing with all these competing demands, then it's almost certain that you will be overwhelmed. It's not that there aren't enough hours in the day. It's that there aren't enough seconds in a minute to deal with the demands of the present. If you don't clearly prioritize your time, if you don't draw a line in the sand, if you can't keep up with the different things that demand your attention, then the media will gladly take over this responsibility for you. The media have no upper limit on this issue—they will try to take over. It's the only way they can keep selling you things.

And that's the key: sales. Are you a passive consumer of your life? Do you numbly follow the hottest, the coolest, the latest things that are being hurled at you at light-speed when you turn on the radio, flick on the TV, or click online? Or do you try to control it? Most consumers have been reduced to nervous, reactive, twitchy purchasing machines who have little awareness and less understanding of the things they are constantly asked to buy. How can anyone forge real independence from all this hoopla?

Priorities by themselves are not enough. They are first principles, they are a plan, but without support they cannot survive. It takes more than good intentions to become truly independent. It takes something that the media will never sell you, something that they are reluctant to acknowledge, much less promote. It takes discipline. Remember discipline? Willfully restraining yourself from doing something that you know is not right, or bad for you, or bad for others—this is not the American commercial creed. Did discipline make us the most obese country in the world? No. Did discipline cause us to become the biggest consumers, and wasters, on the planet? No. Did discipline make you buy the big house, the big car, the big vacation that you probably couldn't afford? No. What, then? They sold it to you. That's all they do. They sell. It's their job. Granted, sales are necessary. But like all things necessary, they must be understood and accepted in moderation. Without moderation, consumption is just an addiction. Without priorities, consumption becomes a reflex. Without values, consumption just becomes another out-of-control process determined to crush you. Without perceiving all the ways that you can be turned into a follower, you can never be independent.

Priorities, values, understanding, and discipline are not easy. They are not quick fixes. They require care and tending. They are the seawall that you must maintain so as not to drown in the information you are exposed to daily. If properly maintained and adjusted, that seawall can save you. It can deflect the more ruinous tides of instant diets, new drugs, wonder machines, and smart technology that make you a consumer-victim in no time. Properly maintained, this wall can protect you, your spouse, your children, your job, your house, and your life. But if you are careless, if you let part of this wall come down…then you are in the hands of others. And they are not looking out for you and yours. Just the opposite. It's in their interest that your life is fragmented, that your attention span is short, that you depend on the media for answers to every question in your life. They will maintain their assault, too, just like waves. "Time and tide wait for no man" was once a truism in a world where the sailing ship was the fastest means of transportation. Now the same thing can be said about a purely man-made creation: the media.

An independent person is the last thing the media want. An independent person can resist fads and trends and make an honest assessment about whether the "latest" thing is really necessary. An independent person is not easily shifted from his or her core values, as opposed to responding instantly to the last thing on display. An independent person is unmoved by the promises of instant remedies to big problems at low cost and in new and improved forms. An independent person insists on having his or her most important needs met in the most economical ways, without sacrificing more than is decent for the services or goods needed.

Faced with this kind of integrity, strength of purpose, and clear-eyed perception of true interest, the collective selling machine that is the media spends imponderable amounts of time and money and energy to split you off into niche markets, consumer groups, and favored demographics. Where are the family values in that? Where are values of any kind? When everything is reduced to the commercial, the important parts of every human's life seem to get left out. Where is true love in the marketplace? Where are compassion, empathy, and sensitivity? You know how these things have all been marketed: love is a diamond, compassion is a greeting card, empathy is a diet tip, and sensitivity is dermabrasion treatment. Shouldn't knowing this make it harder for them to get to us, though?

This brings us to another important element of independence: memory. One of the side effects of being the most "mediatized" country in the world is memory loss. By this, I don't mean birthdays and holidays and other time markers. I mean that we don't seem to remember that the quick fixes of yesterday, so highly touted, didn't solve anything. Does anyone remember thalidomide, the wonder drug that caused untold numbers of birth defects? Or the lobotomy, used for the mentally ill, which made desperate cases hopeless? Or phrenology, which purportedly analyzed personalities by examining the bumps on someone's head? All were once thought to be innovative solutions to terrible problems. All were discredited before we blithely moved on to the next wonder-something that would finally solve the horror of the Next Big Problem.

Clearly, in a society as dedicated to innovation and experimentation as ours, we will fail at times. The drive to find the best solutions to the biggest problems will continue. But the best solution for individuals remains the hallmark of America: independence. Individuals must grasp *independence* with both hands; they must defend it and eventually teach it. Independence, like freedom, cannot be given; it must be taken. And it must be defended. There is no way to maintain your independence if you are unaware of the many ways that it is assaulted every day. People use the word independence casually, referring to it on the Fourth of July. But real independence means having the freedom within oneself to exercise that precious right properly. It is the will to stand out from the crowd by saying "No." It is often the most difficult thing one can do, because it means willing to be singled out. It means willing to be "different." Occasionally it means being criticized. It's the price that must be paid, because the alternative is a loss of individuality, of freedom, and of will. Did our forefathers fight so hard all those years ago to be turned into nervous, muted "consumers"? Is that what it was all about? I don't think so, and I bet you agree with me.

If you want to be an independent thinker, you cannot be afraid to look at the most basic assumptions you have about the world and ask hard questions. Will buying this make me any happier, healthier, wiser? Will it make me more free or less free? How much time will this new "time-saving" product actually save? Or is it just another way to get me to buy, buy, buy? Even more basic questions need to be asked, and every day. Am I happy? Why? What causes me to be happy? What prevents me from being happy? What can I do about it? Questions like these are much more likely to lead you onto productive paths of thinking, to new ways of envisioning and attacking your problems, than wondering what new thing you should buy.

Independent thinking is something we praise in our historical leaders—how this or that person resisted going along with the crowd, resisted the outrage of critics, and led the way to a better future. What about today's nonconformists? How are they actually treated? Today, an entire network of ready-made reflexes exists, designed to put people down who insist on their own way. From the time we are in school we realize that conformity pays dividends. The most popular people set trends, and others follow. But are they really setting trends—new ways of doing things—or are they just enforcing a status quo that they don't really understand? Is it really necessary for "everyone" to wear the right clothes and sport the approved haircut, listen to the music selected for them and watch the movies and shows that they watch? Or is "popularity" a code for conformity? Isn't that just the same as passively accepting mediocrity?

Beware of trends. They tend to serve one commercial interest or another. Usually developed, refined, packaged, and promoted to lure you in and "sell" you. The connotation is chilling—now, in the language of sales, "selling" people is considered a virtue. It may just be a trick of language, but selling someone should give everyone pause. What is being sold? More importantly, who is being sold? How many people have been willing to give up their birthright of independence for the sake of conformity? And what do they gain? Temporary acceptance? A quick acknowledgment that they "fit in"? Invitations to the "right" places? It seems a high price to pay for something that is guaranteed to need replacing or updating in…ten minutes.

Since this system begins in youth, it is important to keep a close eye on children. They are the biggest victims. Now, to an extent children cannot be allowed freedom and independence. They lack the maturity and judgment to make good decisions. But in your absence, your children are being told what to buy, what to enjoy, and what they think they need. If they are not carefully taught and guided, they will become dependent on these messages to make up their minds. And these messages, as I said, are not benign.

Being part of this world requires that we do our best to make it the best of all possible worlds. This means constant vigilance against the nasty influences we are exposed to daily. Participating in freedom, rather than the marketing of it, requires that we be conscious of all its aspects. People are free to pursue their own (hopefully) enlightened self-interest, but companies are, too. They will do their best to "capture" you—as a market, of course—and "sell" you. Sometimes their wares are good: computers and cell phones are necessary, like it or not. But sometimes they only want to sell you something because they know you will buy it, whether your interest is enlightened or not. And they will prey on your worst fears to do this. (Fen-phen, anyone?) In the most extreme cases, these "sales" can kill you. But even when a product doesn't kill you, companies know that you can be sold on something like it in the future. They think you can be made into someone who reacts to the latest stimulus of fear, insecurity, or vanity. You are no longer an individual at that point, but a market.

This situation leads some people to overreact. They start growing their own food or making their own clothes as a sign of extreme nonconformity. This is largely pointless. Our biggest decisions remain our commercial decisions, and it is possible to spend your money wisely and well, promoting your family's health and happiness without having to grow your own potatoes. And it is impossible, as well, to get rid of advertising and promotion. They are as much a part of the modern world as the automobile. They are the scorpion on the frog, from the old fable. They don't mean to sting you; it's just the way they are.

But independence of mind, spirit, and action are the legacy of America. Are you willing to trade that in without any resistance? Will you go quietly? History suggests that many of you, the ones who strive for true independence, will not. And history suggests that, for those of you who achieve independence, the future is an open field you can advance in at your own pace, in your own time, and following your own path.

Enjoy that future. It's not an easy thing to achieve, real freedom to choose. Once accomplished, though, no one has ever regretted it. Be your own leader. How will you know that you've arrived? After a period of being alone, you will notice that your happiness has attracted a crowd. And they have a lot of questions for you.

"To fulfill yourself is the most unique, the most powerfully addictive, and the most easily disrupted thing you can attempt."

"I REJECT LIMITS—PERIOD." —David Foster

I HAVE BEEN IN the dark for more than forty years. What else would you call the life of a record producer? It's my job to wring music from the air, to make sounds coordinate in ways that did not exist before, to see to it that every ounce of talent, energy, and creativity is harnessed to a single guiding vision that can communicate itself to people all over the world.

I have lived and worked and loved music so long that it has become my first language, one that transcends any spoken or written words I could offer. That is why I feel that whatever I might communicate on the page can only be a fraction of the story. But I do believe that everyone should review his or her own life and make every effort to hit the highest notes. As Socrates said, "The unexamined life is not worth living." I have led a life that I promise has been completely worth leading, but I'll let you be the judge of that.

To date, I have been awarded fifteen Grammys and was nominated forty-four times. I've sold half a billion records and launched the careers of some of the biggest superstars the world has ever known.

When I was four years old, my mother sat down at our piano and played a single note. "That's an E!" I shouted from the kitchen. I didn't realize it at the time, but this little statement would turn out to be the turning point of my life. My parents began testing me and sure enough, without anyone understanding how I had learned it or when exactly it was that I knew the scales and basics of music, the fact was undeniable: I had perfect pitch. This meant that I could tell if a note was off by even the tiniest bit. This ability has been the touchstone, guide, and whip of my life. I have never stopped trying to share that terrible perfection with artists, musicians, and audiences. It compels me every day. It will wake me tomorrow.

After that discovery, it was just a matter of time until my parents had me training seriously. By the time I was ten, I had four years of classical training. By thirteen, I was booking weddings, social events, and the like—I was sought after. I entered the University of Washington that same year and I've never looked back. That is, I understood as far back as when my age could be measured in single digits what it was I was going to do. It wasn't clear to me exactly how or when or with whom or what style it would take, but I did understand that my life would be permanently and inextricably bound up with music. I had no idea just how far that would take me. I remember having a thought around the age of fourteen or fifteen that I might be able to make a pretty good living playing in the clubs of suburban Vancouver, at least for a while.

This was a time of great change in music. While I was in school, a British band called the Beatles emerged on the scene and hit me like a meteorite out of the blue. Their impact was so powerful to people of a certain generation that it still stuns me to realize that many don't really understand who they were or how important they were. To say that they were an earthquake or a tsunami or a lightning bolt still manages to grossly understate their significance. I can tell you their impact on me: I gave up classical music completely. Rock 'n' roll became the *only* music—to play, to discuss, and to write.

This is where my thinking was when I became the keyboardist for Chuck Berry at the ripe old age of seventeen.

The 1960s being what they were—a completely different planet than the one we now inhabit—it was not too much of a stretch for my parents to allow me to go on tour with Mr. Berry. We crossed the United States and then went to England. As tours do, this one broke up, and when it ended, everyone went home. Everyone but me. My parents had spent their entire life savings to buy me a keyboard. They gave me a hall pass and their blessing to rock the world from the U.K. I was not going to go home a disappointment, so I stayed in England and looked for work.

It was a bleak time, but a time that I now remember as filled with hope. I knew that I could play, and even though I barely had enough to eat, I was determined to hang around long enough for someone to discover this fact.

It seems crazy now. I was just a teenager without money or prospects. I had exactly one tour under my belt. I barely shaved, but somehow I knew something that no one else did—I knew I could really play. When I think of the many turns my career has taken since then, it is startling for me to grasp this early confidence. At the time, the explosion of the British Invasion was dominating popular music like nothing anyone had ever seen before. The Beatles, the Rolling Stones, the Who, Led Zeppelin, Eric Clapton, Rod Stewart—the names go on and on; they play on the radio every day to this day. I was a Canadian teenager from outside Vancouver—not a household name by any stretch. But I persevered. I went to the clubs and listened to the bands. I got to know people.

Eventually, I became a session man—a keyboardist who would play with anyone. In time, I played with everyone: McCartney, Harrison, Rod Stewart, and many, many others. It didn't take me very long to understand that just playing was not enough. I wanted to be in charge of the music itself. This meant being a producer. At the time, many people told me that what I wanted was a step down. How could I want to go behind the scenes when I was already onstage and in the studio with legends? Frankly, I really wasn't sure of what I was doing.

A powerful lesson from an undisputed master put me straight. After I had produced my first or second record, I had a conversation with Quincy Jones. I confessed to him that I had just finished producing a record but that I was dissatisfied. I described the situation to him: "I just finished this record, but only two or three of the songs are good." What followed seemed like an eternal pause. Finally, he spoke. "Are you telling me that your name is going on a record you don't really support?" I swallowed hard and uttered, "Yes." He said, "Is that your name on the record? Does it say David Foster? That means *you* are the producer and no one else. That means *you* are responsible for every second of music that's on that record. If there are only two or three songs that you liked, then you had better get back in there and see to it that that record deserves to have your name—and only yours—as the producer."

Needless to say, that exchange has stayed with me every day since. I realized that there are compromises in life that must be made, that not everything turns out the way you plan, but there are limits to compromise. Some things you don't compromise. When you produce art of any kind, or for that matter when you produce anything that you put your name on, you are responsible for its presentation, its form, and its content. You are—no one else. This is what made me want to be a producer in the first place—the desire to control every aspect of the music, from conception to execution. It was not vanity that drove me to become a perfectionist in the studio. If it was anything, it was the need to fulfill the music that existed only in my head.

That meant achieving something that no one else can really experience: the development and expression of my inner vision. The complete flourishing of what was once only a seed of an idea into an entire plant, complete with flowers. To fulfill yourself is the most unique, the most powerfully addictive, and the most easily disrupted thing you can attempt. It is routinely something that others protest about, complain about, and often try to impede, wittingly or unwittingly. And yet, there it lies—fulfillment. Achieving it even once leaves you with the perfect desire to do only one thing: do it again. Few, if any, human actions lead to this euphoric feeling of achievement. Some are forced to live a lifetime after experiencing it only once. This is so common in music that the term "one-hit wonder" has become known in every industry, though it originated in ours. Others chase it and chase it. I'm a chaser. And because I have chased and chased, I have never been able to rest on my laurels. I have created opportunities for myself that might not otherwise have become available.

Fulfillment is a dangerous drug. Once you've had it, it's difficult to settle for less. The fact that you have created something wonderful where before there was nothing…this is a fantastically satisfying experience, while also potentially disastrous. What if you can't do it again? What if you were just lucky? After fifteen Grammy awards, I can assure you that these questions are not just academic. They are the driving force behind much of what I have done and continue to do. It is not a casual effort I make. It is the expression of a vision that consumes and impels and requires me to try harder, to seek out new artists, to push them and myself beyond our "reasonable" limits. I reject limits—period. If I believe that after great effort and lots of time the vision is not achieved, we start over. I learned Quincy's lesson well. I apply it to everything I do.

As the 1970s gave way to the 1980s, I found myself less a conductor of my career and more a channel for it. That is, I could not stop working. There seemed unlimited possibilities for me, possibilities that required my focus, attention, and follow-through every minute of every day. When you are in the grip of a muse, it is impossible to free yourself from its demands. I worked day and night, week in and week out, month after month, year after year. In my case, self-expression through others became so consuming that I was unable to even consider balance of any kind. I was not on a treadmill, I was on the world's biggest hamster wheel—frantically running and running and running with no end in sight. I might take breaks, but they were never what you would call vacations. I always heard the bells in the distance calling me back to action. And what action it was!

I produced music in just about every venue that existed. I worked with what seemed like literally everyone—Barbra Streisand, Celine Dion, Mariah Carey, Michael Bublé…the list goes on and on. With every success, with every gold record, with every Grammy, I was happy, true; but I also felt that there remained so much to be done, so many more people to work with, that it never remotely appeared to be enough. There was no end in sight.

There are people who are satisfied with accomplishment. They look forward to ending their efforts, to retirement and "the good life." I've never seen it that way. Granted, mine is not the average course of a life. I've been lucky. I've been blessed. I've been fulfilled many times in many ways. But despite this success, I remain driven. I know that many people feel the same way about their lives, that they are not ready to stop doing what they have always done.

I have always felt that it is not about what one has accomplished but how one *feels* about that accomplishment. *Is that it? Am I happy now? Is that enough?* To me, the answer is an obvious NO! I believe that it is this quest for more—for more complete fulfillment—that has driven me to continue. I think a lot of people feel this way but they don't seize a chance to act on it.

I'm lucky to be an independent thinker. I constantly look for opportunities and create situations to realize even more dreams—not only my own, but the dreams of others.

Connecting to other artists has kept me creative; it has made me feel renewed in my abilities, my art, and myself.

People have the capacity to do things that they can't even imagine. I am proof! I've come a long way from thinking that I might make a living playing the clubs of Victoria, British Columbia. I'm still looking for new talent. I'm still trying to achieve a new perfection. I will never be satisfied completely. There will be successes and disappointments, upsides and downsides, but one thing has been with me from the beginning, and I suspect it will be with me until the end: creating music is creating life, and I, for one, am not finished with either.

**“Have you shaped your destiny,
or have circumstances shaped you?”**

THE LAW OF THOUGHT AND SUPPLY

THROUGHOUT HISTORY THE GREAT thinkers of the world have repeated the same theme over and over: You are living the life you have created. Many different philosophies, political systems, and laws of accountability have embodied this in their own way. Everything that is in your life, you have attracted in your life. With each passing moment, with each passing thought, with each action no matter how trivial or profound, the law of thought and supply repeats this theme like a mantra: The things you think about have made you exactly who you are right now. What you continue to think about will determine who you will become tomorrow, next month, next year, and for the rest of your life.

It is a major challenge to comprehend, and certainly to accept, that whatever thoughts pass through your mind become the blueprint for your future. After all, you think a lot of things every day that don't seem momentous: *Wouldn't tomato soup be good tonight? I wonder where I can find a good phone? Was that shade of blue the best one for that dress?* The truth is that these thoughts, like the 60,000 other ones you have on a typical day, are determining your fate. Whatever you are thinking about, you are attracting to you. It is accurate to state that your thoughts determine whether you will fail or succeed.

Despite our brains firing thoughts while we're awake and asleep at the rate of 60,000 a day, it is clear that ninety percent of these thoughts are subconscious and seemingly out of our control. Imagine being behind the wheel of a car, or flying a plane, or caring for an infant, or making an important business decision while functioning at a ten percent level of awareness. While functioning on autopilot is unimaginable under virtually any circumstance in our day-to-day lives, this autopilot is actually the norm. Sound far-fetched? Think about just how many things you do every day without thinking about them. "Autopilot thoughts" kick in as a response to stimuli in any given environment that you find yourself in, whether it's a red light, a crying child, or an alarm clock.

Automatic thoughts can be positive or negative; they can propel you to success or tear you down. They guide your thought patterns, attitudes, and behaviors. The feedback you receive from them validates those thoughts. It's a perpetual cycle with its own built-in system for maintaining itself. You are not even aware of this reinforcement most of the time—until circumstances force you to do what your subconscious mind resists, which is examining itself. You are trapped in a cycle until you reach a level of awareness that requires you to reexamine your own thought patterns. Only then can you instigate change; only then can you seize control of your own mind and alter what you choose to think about.

Why is your thinking life so vital? You may be thinking that the last thing you need right now is more responsibility and demands on your time for self-improvement and self-actualization. As if working hard, exercising, eating right, and all the pressures of modern life aren't enough; now you must take full, conscious charge of your vastly numerous and random thoughts!

Let's put it in perspective: Everything else in your life is like putting the cart before the horse. Your thinking life is the mental nucleus and DNA of what is actualized in your world. What is the point of taking care of your body if counterproductive thinking is making you emotionally unfulfilled, mentally drained, and physically ill?

Researchers now claim that more than eighty-five percent of the illnesses that plague people in our modern society are a direct result of their thinking life, and less than fifteen percent are actually attributable to diet, environment, and genetics. This is a consensus we can no longer afford to ignore. Think about it—if this is true, then our greatest efforts are going toward a fraction of the problem. And we would be ignoring the obvious conclusion: thinking is the most crucial aspect of health. If this is true, shouldn't we focus on our thinking? Shouldn't we look at our thinking as a cause of our problems, as well as the opportunity to solve them? What good does it do us to put enormous efforts into research, treatment, and training if it amounts to a Band-Aid on a bullet wound?

We are experiencing an epidemic of toxic emotions. Research shows that fear alone triggers some 1,400 physical and chemical responses and activates more than thirty hormones. Research has also shown that it is possible to control fear by confronting its root causes. If it is possible to control fear, then shouldn't it be possible to control other toxic emotions? Wouldn't that have a profound impact on our health? And wouldn't that in turn have an effect on our happiness, our ability to confront our challenges, and the outcomes of our efforts? There are intellectual and medical reasons for living a mentally sound life. There are spiritual reasons for living a rewarding and prosperous life. To be healthy, happy, and wealthy is your responsibility as well as your birthright. The good news? It is in your power—and no else's—to achieve this.

The final frontier is the mind. Most of the time we take it for granted. Regardless of who you are, where you are, or what you are doing, your brain is conducting about 400 billion actions at any given moment, and you are aware of fewer than 2,000 of them. Every single carefully orchestrated action has a chemical and an electrical aspect that triggers all your emotions.

You can think of your brain as a sophisticated factory that produces chemicals corresponding to the thoughts you think and the emotions you generate. Depending on the thoughts you think, the chemicals released will benefit you or harm you. Emotions known to cause the most physical and mental harm include vengefulness, resentment, anger, hostility, rage, depression, worry, anxiety, frustration, fear, guilt, and grief. Even with modern, high-tech medical intervention and an endless variety of drugs and homeopathic remedies, most of the chronic illnesses plaguing society—diabetes, hypertension, heart disease, strokes, migraines, infectious diseases, allergies, and depression—are actually on the increase, not decline. We have reached a point where one conclusion is clear: depression increases our risk of heart disease and cancer, the first and second leading causes of death, respectively.

The good news is that the opposite is also true: positive emotions release healing chemicals. Unfortunately, instead of embracing this obvious solution to the widespread problem of depression, the medical community has embraced an endless series of "happy pills," drugs that artificially change the brain's chemistry to make you feel more content—for a while. Instead of detoxifying the mind and body by changing harmful thinking patterns and poor lifestyle choices, we bombard the brain with mind-altering drugs that temporarily relieve suffering at best, and cause long-term harm at worst.

Much was made of Tom Cruise's passionate stance against psychiatric drugs when he made his views publicly known in response to Brooke Shields's need to alleviate her postpartum depression with antidepressants. The media (sponsored by the pharmaceutical companies) came down on him like an airplane crashing from the skies. They portrayed him as callous and unsupportive of women in general, dismissive of a problem and a syndrome that plagues women in every walk of life. Scientology aside, Tom's statements were informed and accurate. Many psychotropic drugs are prescribed with scant knowledge of their long-term effects. While some may not have appreciated his tone, he comprehends the need to understand how potentially harmful psychotropic drugs are, and how much power we actually possess to make ourselves physically and emotionally healthy.

Today it is far easier to pop a pill (or a few) than work on the emotions that shoot through us in the battlefield of the mind. These emotional responses represent the shadow responses of our thoughts, and it is our thoughts, our thinking lives, that determine the reality we experience every day. Once we accept that emotions affect how our bodies respond to stimuli, we must also accept responsibility for creating the conditions for optimal health or degenerating illness, for success or failure. We must literally make ourselves well or sick, rich or poor. Your brain might bring you to the brink of destruction after years of stinkin' thinkin', but given half a fighting chance, it can begin to recover on its own almost immediately. Remember—you can bury your emotions, but you will be burying something alive that will eventually start digging its way out.

Where are your thoughts right now? To what point in your life have you brought yourself? Have you shaped your destiny, or have circumstances shaped you? Do you recognize the voices you have allowed to control you, to limit you? Are you conscious of the many ways that you can limit yourself, and of the many chances you have to escape these limits?

Let me tell you a story. When I was in college, my first American literature professor called me into his office at the end of the semester. The disheveled elderly professor sat behind his desk and kindly asked me to sit down. He removed his glasses slowly and rubbed his hound-dog face. He appeared to be in agony.

"Look," he finally spoke, "you are a very bright and nice young lady. You are very pretty and well mannered, and you will most likely have a decent life. But," he continued, giving his face a fresh rub, "I've been reading your commentaries and essays, and somebody has got to tell you that you just can't have what you wish for in life."

I raised my left eyebrow and squinted at him. "What I mean to say is this. It's all fine and noble to have dreams and aspirations—grand ambitions—but yours are so lofty that they could never possibly come true. What I am telling you is that you're setting yourself up for some serious failure and major heartbreak when you realize that dreams like yours, by someone like you, just don't come true in the real world."

I observed the poor man. Granted, he was over sixty and had some life experience, and I was just eighteen, but I remember thinking, sympathetically, "You poor slob. What a wreck of a human being you turned into." Nevertheless, I stood up, thanked the professor for his concern and, recognizing it was the best advice he was capable of, left the office. I walked out the door shaking my head to myself. *What a misguided soul.*

The professor wasn't entirely wrong. But it was a lucky thing for me that I didn't know how to limit my "lofty" thoughts. I've endured a challenging and sometimes brutal journey on all the roads I've traveled. But I have learned something I hope to pass on, especially in the final chapter of this book: When the circumstances of your life give you virtually no options and you've only got your imagination to bank on, your reality can become every bit as great as your imagination.

"The reason man may become the master of his own destiny is because he has the power to influence his own subconscious mind," Napoleon Hill stated. Our thoughts make us the individuals we are. Rene Descartes, the seventeenth-century French philosopher, claimed that one's thoughts established one's existence. He proclaimed: "I think, therefore I am." He was telling us that no matter what outside agency might influence us, the proof of our existence was not external, but internal, in that most internal of all processes: thinking.

Today more than ever, our thoughts are influenced and manipulated by outside forces, especially the media. John Berger, in *Ways of Seeing*, explained, "The way we see things is affected by what we know or what we believe." In other words, what we see and hear is already subjective in our minds. Some claim that, in reality, we no longer possess the possibility of discerning anything with our own minds because we observe things and distinguish them by what we have already been taught or programmed to perceive. Why aren't we then training ourselves to defend our minds from distorting, negative messages? Because there are many powerful interests that try to shape those messages for us, to drain us of our free will and the independence that Descartes teaches us is the hallmark of our humanity.

Although political, economic, and cultural interests consistently desire a populace that can be easily controlled, the theme of creating and managing our thoughts and determining our own future has been a timeless leadership principle throughout history. From our most ancient tests to the modern age, the message does not change. Our life is determined by what our thoughts make it. The apostle Paul wrote that "God hath chosen the foolish things of the world to confound the wise; and God hath chosen the weak things of the world to confound the things that are mighty." In other words, the path to our own healing is sometimes blocked by the so-called wisdom of experts. Darwin stated, "The highest possible stage in moral culture is when we recognize that we ought to control our thoughts." Emerson had the same idea, writing, "Life consists of what a man is thinking all day." The Bible, the greatest textbook on prosperity ever written, offers the ultimate divine promise: "All things are yours" (1 Corinthians 3:21).

Once you comprehend and accept this, you will realize that people, places, conditions, and events simply cannot keep your divinely offered peace, prosperity, and success from you. Once you learn how to employ right-minded thinking as your most powerful source to prosperity, you will understand how all the people and things that have worked against you in the past can actually work for you and propel you to new heights of success and abundance.

King Solomon of Israel, son of David, was the richest man who ever lived. In Proverbs 23:7, he said what many philosophers through the ages have tried to make their own: “As a man thinks within himself, so is he.”

The question remains: who do you think you are?

"You can't sell anything to anyone if you arrive with the attitude that you have been defeated by life."

"SUCCESS UNSHARED IS FAILURE" —JOHN PAUL DEJORIA

WHEN I WAS FOUR or five years old, my mother took my brother and me downtown at Christmastime. We were so impressed with all the stores—Broadway, Bullocks, the May Company—and their displays of decorations and lights. Our eyes were as big as saucers. Then my mother did something that has been with me every day since. She took out a dime and told my brother and me to carry it together and give it to the people ringing bells for the Salvation Army. A dime was a lot of money back then—it was a streetcar ride to Santa Monica, it was two big candy bars—and my brother and I were so impressed with it that we took turns holding it as we walked to the Salvation Army bucket. We went back to my mother and said, "Wow, Mom, that's a lot of money." She smiled. "Yes, I know," she said, "and we could use that dime. But they need it more." Eventually, I boiled this experience down to one phrase: Success unshared is failure. Even when I was homeless and living in my car, I carried this idea with me. I carry it today.

When I got out of the navy in 1964 (I served on the USS *Hornet*) I had a lot of jobs. I sold photocopiers, towels, soap, and eventually encyclopedias. This was the job that taught me what I would most need to know. What did it teach me? Rejection. I had more doors closed on me than on winter chill. And I learned that there was only one thing that could triumph over rejection: determination. If ten doors slammed shut in my face, I grew determined that the eleventh would not. I greeted the eleventh door as if it were the first. That was an important lesson. So many people give up in the face of rejection that I think it has ended more brilliant careers than any other problem. Rejection can be so dispiriting. It saps your will, your energy, and your best ideas. It feels like a repudiation not only of your product but also of you. I've seen this over and over. People take rejection personally. I learned not to. And when the eleventh door would open, I'd remember how I had felt with the first ten. I was determined not to let it stop me. Rejection, I learned, was just another part of business. I could let it get to me or I could use it to spur me on. And I learned another valuable lesson: successful people are the ones who do what unsuccessful people are unwilling to do.

It wasn't just a personal humiliation that I was facing, either. I was so poor that I was homeless, more than once. I had to sell or starve. I remember collecting cans for deposit money to buy macaroni and cheese—with my young son. Is there anything more humbling than hunger? Is there anything more humbling than knowing your son is witnessing what the entire society considers to be failure? These experiences were extremely wrenching and debilitating at the time. But I'm glad I went through them. They were the lessons I learned that kept me from ever getting complacent. There are experiences that everyone goes through that stay with them forever. I've had many, good and bad, but I've never lost sight of the fact that I was trying to do something different; I was trying to change. It didn't always work out the way I wanted, but was that a reason to quit? I couldn't afford to. So I didn't. I realized that the only response to life's rejections was to try again, with new energy. You can't sell anything to anyone if you arrive with the attitude that you have been defeated by life. You can't sell anything to yourself if you feel that way.

I had to go door-to-door with the same enthusiasm regardless of my situation. Every sale was a windfall, every door-slamming a catastrophe. But the attitude had to be the same, no matter the result. I just continued to put out positive energy, positive energy, positive energy. I literally could not afford to be negative. There was so much to be negative about that to go there would have been to spiral into self-doubt, misery, and hopelessness. There was nothing else to do but put my best foot forward. It's amazing what you can accomplish when you don't think you have a choice.

Eventually I worked at *Time* magazine, running a boiler room of salesmen in the circulation department. I was in charge of it by the time I was twenty-six, but I knew that without a college degree I would only rise so far, and that would take years. I decided to go out on my own. How bad could it be? At least I'd be working for myself, I would be my own man, and I wouldn't have to answer to anyone else's idea of what I should be. How did it work out? You guessed it—before it was over I was living in my car again, and divorced. There are a lot of doors out there, after all. The slams were getting familiar, as was my determination to overcome them.

At thirty-five, with no money and fewer prospects, I decided to try the hair products business with a good friend of mine, Paul Mitchell. He knew shampoo and hairdressing; I knew sales. With $700—part of my share was borrowed—we got started, selling door-to-door to salons. This would become the basis of our success—that we lacked the money for advertising. Isn't that ironic? We didn't have the means to "sell" things by mail or through newspapers or magazines or television, so we were forced to reinvent the wheel. We sold ourselves, and by that I mean we sold ourselves as personally responsible for our products. We weren't some faceless corporation that occupied enormous shelf space in every supermarket. We weren't on TV selling beautiful images. We only had ourselves, so that's what we sold. We also had a fantastic product, which made it easy to throw ourselves behind it. We guaranteed that the products would sell, or we would buy them back. We went from salon to salon. In the years we were doing that, I think we got maybe one return. Maybe.

I distilled all that experience—going from homelessness to having a self-sustaining business—into a sales principle I've used ever since: underpromise and overperform. If you do your job twice as well as anyone expects it to be done, it will be remembered. Conversely, if you promise more than you can deliver, that will be remembered, too, and not to your benefit.

When I first began to enjoy success I met a Mexican cleaning lady. Everyone talked about her as being the hardest worker they'd ever seen. In her sixties, she had two jobs and was supporting her whole family. One day I told her that she had done a great job that week, as she had every week, and I told her to take a two-hour lunch break. She stopped cleaning and looked at me, surprised. "Why would I do that?" she asked. I told her that I appreciated all of her work and wanted her to relax for a change. She told me something I never forgot. "I would much rather be productive and earn your appreciation again." For her it was much more important to have gotten the recognition than to stop putting in that effort. It was the effort that gave her the self-esteem that nothing and no one could take from her. This was another important lesson for me about the nature of work. If you do your best at whatever job you have, you know that what you do is worth doing.

When I had graduated from my car to an apartment, and could finally start paying bills on time and enjoying luxuries like car insurance, I decided for the first time in a long time to go out to dinner. I went to a Mexican restaurant, not expensive, but one that I liked. I was delighted to be able to order from the right side of the menu without looking at the prices. As I was deciding what to eat, I looked around the restaurant. I saw a group of inner-city kids, blacks and Latinos. They were poor, these children, and the mothers looking after them were clearly struggling with the menu. I knew the feeling. Many times I had to look carefully at the prices on a menu before ordering. I went to the waiter in the back of the restaurant and asked him to tell these women to order anything and everything they wanted for the kids, and that it was all paid for, plus tip. I told him not to tell them who was buying. I was sitting three feet behind one of the ladies when the waiter whispered in her ear. She got up and scanned the room, looking right past me. Then she announced in a loud, evangelical voice, "Whoever you are, may God bless you. You have no idea what you did for me and the children." The place went absolutely silent. I got a cold chill throughout my body. It was the greatest high I've ever had in my life. I remembered my mother and the Salvation Army dime. I remembered being homeless. I remembered the doors slamming shut in my face. And I cemented that lesson into my soul, this time. *Success unshared is failure*.

Within a few years I was rich. Our products were the best of their kind in the world, and at every opportunity we made them even better. We were eco-friendly before anyone had heard of that. We compensated all of our workers generously without it being mandated by any government or union. Paul Mitchell and I were determined. We weren't driven to be rich, really. We just used our success as proof that we were right—our products were the best, they delivered the most, and they satisfied our customers. In business, having a good product makes it a lot easier to go out and sell it with conviction. And when you have a bad product, well, those get sold all the time, too, but I doubt they provide anyone with any real satisfaction, even if people make a lot of money on them.

Our goal was always customer satisfaction. If we could really deliver on our promises, then we knew we would be compensated. As Paul was dying of pancreatic cancer a few years later, he told me that if Paul Mitchell products could just sell $100 million a year, he would look down and smile. He didn't mean that the money was important—just that it was measurable proof that we were right, that our products were so good that the world deserved to have them. Paul died in 1989. Needless to say, a few years later we were making well over $100 million a year, and we've never looked back.

Sticking to that plan has allowed us to grow even more, to the point where I could celebrate the twentieth anniversary of my homelessness by buying a seat on the New York Stock Exchange. But that was not the goal. Like I said: success unshared is failure. I never forgot that restaurant, or that mother who stood up in it. My charitable organizations, and those I contribute to and work for, are responsible for feeding children all over the world, for clearing landmines left over from wars and helping their victims, and for saving whales and dolphins at sea. I'm on the board of the Creative Coalition, which keeps jobs in America, and I am working on other philanthropies and organizations every day. Why? Because success unshared…you get the idea.

But it's not just a bumper sticker. I have come to believe that it is a real human institution. I believe in God, but I also believe in not waiting around for His mercy. Humans need to connect to other humans, and in meaningful ways. If you perceive human suffering, it is not enough to pay lip service to the problem. People spend a lot of time assigning blame for the world's problems. How many of those problems would still exist if we all spent that time doing something about them instead?

For that matter, it seems to me that people have it within their means to tackle all kinds of problems successfully, and not just the obvious ones like poverty. People get tangled up in their own lives in ways that lend themselves to some simple, though sometimes painful, fixes. Especially about the work they do. If you aren't happy doing what you do for a living, change it. Believe me, however difficult that sounds, life is too short to be doing something just to pay the bills. There are so many more opportunities for people than there used to be, so many more ways to express their true abilities, that I think it's a shame that more people don't avail themselves of these opportunities more often. When I see how different the world is today from the one I grew up in, I am always astonished. Forty years ago the words *software* and *engineer* would never be found in the same sentence, and if they were, they might have described someone who made plastics. Thirty years ago a "programmer" was someone who decided what was going to be on the TV schedule. Twenty years ago the "Internet" might have been a hair product. Ten years ago, well, you get the idea.

Today, more than ever, anything is possible. There will always be tough economic times, as well as boom times. But the principles that sustain you are not subject to boom-and-bust economic cycles. The ideas and ideals that you develop over a lifetime are not pegged to the Dow Jones index. Your sense of self-worth cannot be purchased. Your reactions to adversity make you who you are. Your recovery from adversity is more important than any victory.

People don't give themselves enough credit for the abilities they have, and they definitely spend far, far too much time focusing on their problems. I can tell you that no matter how difficult your circumstances, no matter how dire the situation you find yourself in, others have it worse. People recover from unbelievable hardships, from brutal lives forced on them through no fault of their own. People overcome disease, devastation, war, loss of limbs, of family members, of self-respect. People are built to overcome. But many are beaten down, needlessly, by things they believe are out of their control. I am here to tell you that there is always one thing you can control: your future. What you decide to do about your problems, and then going out and doing it, will do more to shape your future than all the hand-wringing in the world.

Does any one person have all the answers? Of course not. But the only way things have ever gotten better is by appreciating the past and determining to change the future. Clinging to things that no longer serve any purpose is one way people make sure they will be forced to confront the same old problems all over again. If you don't try to change your world, you can always look forward to more of the same. For most of us, that won't do.

How can I say this? How have I come to that conclusion? What makes me think this advice is good? Simple: I've been there and I've done that.

Go ahead. Try it.

“Poverty and shame shall be to him that refuses instruction (Proverbs 13:18).”

ALL THINGS ARE YOURS

THERE IS NOTHING NOBLE or spiritual about poverty—or, for that mater, about the lack of anything. In fact, poverty is a spirit—an evil spirit. It is also a sin, frequently a crime, and always undignified, regardless of what we have been taught to believe in places of worship, Christian schools, Sunday school, or by grandma. So many intelligent and God-fearing people seem to be uncertain about whether prosperity is a blessing or a curse!

It's safe to say that poverty has been, and always will be, the cause of the vast majority of crime, sickness, and hatred, as well as most of the negative and destructive actions and effects imposed on people, often by themselves. It's a form of insanity; it's hell on earth for those who are ignorant of who God is and how the Creator operates. King Solomon felt such an epidemic of ignorance on this issue that he found it vital to declare: "Poverty and shame shall be to him that refuses instruction" (Proverbs 13:18). This sentiment is echoed throughout the Bible, as in Hosea 4:6, when God said, "My people are destroyed for lack of knowledge."

I was born in the former Communist Yugoslavia where in school I was instructed to be faithful to the State and the State would take care of me. In Catholic school in America, I was taught to be faithful to "the one and only" holy Catholic Church and that God would reward me in heaven. In business and personal relationships, most people told me to put my trust, time, and resources in them and I would succeed—eventually. Everybody told me to make sacrifices and that if I did, I would be rewarded in the long run. Most of these instructions did not feel good or natural, but I chose to be obedient and dutiful and I obeyed, as expected. I reasoned that surely my elders and those in positions of authority knew better. I reasoned that surely they knew what was best for me.

Needless to say, at some point, intellectual and emotional percolating begins to take place, no matter how suppressed it has been. Some people ignore it, bury it, or work their life around the queasy feelings and questions that crop up. Sometimes these feelings and questions can become so insistent, so demanding of an audience with us, that they overwhelm our bodies' defenses and bring us down—through illness, depression, or other calamities. We ignore these feelings and theses questions at our peril. They are signposts screaming at us to pay attention to something vital. Too few people begin to seek knowledge on their own. Those who do manage to, given enough understanding and insight, radically alter the course of their lives. For many, however, the prospect of challenging the teachings of their early programming is too daunting. They can't face the possibility that maybe, just maybe, there might be an alternative to poverty, depression, and disappointment. They spend their lives lamenting what they "couldn't have," or what they were "kept from having," and not seeking their own answers or pursuing their own options. They go along with what they are told as children and follow it, blindly, for the rest of their lives. Imagine what would happen if they actually took a good look at those teachings and questioned their premises.

My father's hard-earned money purchased a Catholic education that included angry nuns and uniformly authoritarian priests. They instructed me to live simply and humbly and to prosper just enough not to be a burden to anyone else, so you can only imagine my surprise and intrigue when I first set foot in the Vatican!

Wow! There, nobody has any concept of limitation whatsoever. There are ceilings of pure gold, floors of the finest marble, priceless art, and mind-boggling opulence. There is a greater expenditure and care for corpses than many people enjoy while alive. Now, knowing what I know about the way the law of prosperity operates, that's the way it should be. But that's the way it should be for *all of us* and not just the self-appointed, privileged few. Under these circumstances, the Church (any denomination) becomes the forewarned biblical "oppressor" and not, as advertised, the teacher of God's will for His people. As such, the Church uses God as the "selling point" of its business. This may be good marketing, but it sure is hard on the poor.

So what are you buying? Less than one percent of Christians, Jews, or Muslims have read the Bible or Koran. We rely on middlemen for our knowledge of God's will and for guidance in our lives. Sadly, very few crack open the instruction manual for themselves. As a result, a few have and the rest have not in life. You've heard it said: the rich get richer and the poor get poorer. Is that by accident or design?

If there was any trace in me of believing that poverty holds any virtue, it was wiped away last June. Cardinal Law, the exiled pedophile-protector from Boston, had invited four of us to his private residence at Santa Maria Majore Basilica in Rome. Vatican officials had arranged for an extraordinary private tour beforehand. We joined the cardinal for lunch in his apartment. Seated next to him, I observed his mild manner and humble demeanor. He spoke of sacrifices, of his service to the Church, and of his seemingly genuine awe that more than a million young people had come to the Vatican when Pope John Paul II passed away. "We didn't know what to do in order to get them into the Church," he said. He and the Church were plainly caught off guard that a bewildered modern youth was filled with spiritual hunger, while the church merely offered up religion.

If I didn't know any better—about his exceptional childhood, his position and power in the Church, and his exceedingly privileged life—his performance might have convinced me that he could have been a simple priest from the mountains of Herzegovina. There were several nuns in his service who were brought in from Bulgaria. (They brought us a bottle of wine from Bulgaria to give to Nicola Bulgari, the famous jeweler with whom we were dining that night. The good cardinal explained to them that Mr. Bulgari was not Bulgarian.) "If it wasn't for the sisters," he spoke softly, "I don't know how I would manage."

I had to chew the soggy string beans a few extra times as I tried to imagine just how I could be sitting in the penthouse of a priceless landmark filled with incalculable wealth that is owned by the most powerful Church on earth—one billion members strong—and one of its chiefs was crying poor. I suppose it was the warm-up act. As all who are burdened with the care of national treasures and vast estates know, it takes money and lots of it to keep it going—and they should benefit from the prosperity of those who have it. The tenders of the flock, the shepherds of the Church, did not suffer the same poverty that was the lot of generations of true believers. On the contrary, the humility they professed may have existed in their demeanor, but not their surroundings. In a world of flocks, it pays to be the shepherd. Especially the shepherd who pretends to be a member of the humblest flock.

The Cardinal reminded his lunch guests of this burden, and especially of the current renovation of the Sistine Chapel, as the tiramisu was served. I spied him eyeballing the Bulgari eighteen-carat flawless yellow diamond on my finger. I knew what he was thinking…and for the first time in my life I had absolutely *no* guilt. That little ring has since become a tangible reminder for me, not of my wealth, which is nothing compared to the wealth of the Church, but of the hypocrisy of a system that has endured for millennia—poverty for the many. If I hadn't experienced it firsthand I don't know that I would ever have had as sharp a reminder of the many, many ways people have been fooled about wealth over the centuries.

The men of the Bible were extremely prosperous and among the wealthiest of their times. Even though Jesus was described as being born poor, nothing could be further from the truth. But even if He was poor at birth, He certainly wasn't poor after the Wise Men came to visit and left Him with gold, frankincense, and myrrh. By the way, nowhere in the Bible does it state there were "three" Wise Men, as has often been taught. It was more likely a caravan: it may have been more than 100 men for all we know. As the Bible makes clear, they deposited great wealth with the child. Jesus lived prosperously and preached prosperity even though religion has succeeded in portraying Him otherwise throughout the ages. He appointed a tax collector as an apostle—naming him treasurer to handle all of the apostles' finances; they even paid taxes to the Roman government. Clearly, money was on Jesus' mind. He understood its importance. And he was willing to assert that, in fact, there was another way of looking at things. He understood that poverty may be self-generated, but he also understood that wealth wasn't all it was cracked up to be.

Jesus is portrayed in common robes, but His was no ordinary garment of the day. In fact, His seamless robe was deemed valuable enough for the Roman soldiers to fight over at the cross. One of the wealthiest men of Arimathea, Joseph, then begged Pilate for Jesus' body and buried it in his own extravagant tomb.

Virtually all of the great men of the Bible were either born wealthy, earned great wealth, or had access to money, goods, and services whenever the need arose. Most of them would be, by today's standard, on the Forbes list of the richest men in the world.

Abraham ("The Lord had blessed Abraham in all things," Genesis 24:1); Isaac ("And it came to pass, after the death of Abraham, that God blessed his son Isaac," Genesis 25:11); Jacob ("Thus the man became exceedingly prosperous and had large flocks, female and male servants, and camels and donkeys," Genesis 30:43); Joseph (A former slave-boy and prisoner, Joseph became the second most powerful man in Egypt according to Genesis 45:13); Job ("His possessions were seven thousand sheep, three thousand camels, five hundred yoke of oxen, five hundred female donkeys, and a very large household, so that this man was the greatest of the people of the East," Job 1:1–3; "Now the Lord blessed the latter days of Job more than his beginning, for he had fourteen thousand sheep, six thousand camels, one thousand yoke of oxen, and one thousand female donkeys," Job 42:12); Daniel, who prospered during the regime of four Babylonian Kings (Nebuchadnezzar "promoted Daniel and gave him many great gifts, and he made him ruler over the whole province of Babylon, and chief administrator over all the wise men of Babylon," Daniel 2:48); Boaz, a wealthy landowner and direct descendant of King David ("There was a relative of Naomi's husband, a man of great wealth, of the family of Elimelech. His name was Boaz," Ruth 2:1); David, who started out as a shepherd boy and became Israel's greatest king and one of her wealthiest men; Solomon (Israel's wealthiest king, who "surpassed all the kings of the earth in riches and wisdom," 1 Kings 10:23); Jehoshaphat ("The Lord established the kingdom in his hand; and all Judah gave presents to Jehoshaphat and he had riches and honor in abundance," 2 Chronicles 17:35); and Hezekiah ("Hezekiah had very great riches and honor. And he made himself treasures for silver, for gold, for precious stones, for spices, for shields, and for all kinds of desirable items; storehouses for the harvest of grain, wine, and oil; and stalls for all kinds of livestock, and folds for flocks. Moreover he provided cities for himself, and possessions of flocks and herds in abundances, for God had given him very much property," 2 Chronicles 32:27–29). Yes, these great men of God would be classified as multibillionaires today.

Proverbs 22:7 states, "The rich rule over the poor, and the borrower is the servant to the lender." But just in case you're not absolutely sure, "Money answers everything," according to Ecclesiastes 10:19. Then why are so many people taught that seeking great success and wealth is somehow amoral, ungodly, and egocentric?

Perhaps because the lender is so often the oppressor of the poor. But that is not a commandment. In 1 Timothy 6:17–18, it is explained: "Command those who are rich in this present age not to be haughty, nor to trust in uncertain riches but in the living God, who gives us richly all things to enjoy. Let them do good, that they be rich in good works, ready to give, willing to share."

When all is said and done, you do not honor God or benefit yourself by settling for less and accepting limitations. The concept of "poverty and penance" as the road to salvation was shoved down the throats of the masses when religion first arose. In the Middle Ages, the feudal systems secured wealth only for the select few. Hence poverty was promoted as a great virtue, by design, in order to keep the people poor. The mentality of poverty swept the globe and it continues to keep people oppressed to this day.

The hypocrisy of many religious leaders is precisely in the way they either downplay wealth or praise poverty. To make poverty palatable to the masses, they seem to make being poor a virtue. And yet what is a greater assault on human virtue than poverty? Men of wealth have often been great philanthropists who gave their money away, sometimes in the hope of avoiding the camel-through-the-eye-of-a-needle problem. But those who are truly wealthy are those who have lived a generous life, sharing their knowledge, their experience, and their creativity with others without thought of recompense. If you have lived a life that includes real generosity, then it will be compensated immensely.

There is no bottom line to true generosity; it is not an unpaid debt; it is truly its own reward. Poverty is a circumstance, poverty is a trial, poverty is painful, poverty is many things—but it is *not* a permanent condition. Envisioning the possibility of getting out of poverty, of obtaining wealth, is not just an exercise in wish-fulfillment. It is imperative for life. But like so many things, it requires that you free yourself from the bonds of the past. It requires that you see yourself as something more than the "target market" for some merchandiser's products or services. It requires that you see yourself as the heir to the accumulated knowledge and ability of generations of your forefathers, who certainly had to overcome greater difficulties than you will probably ever face.

This is an abundant universe. There is more than enough to go around. We can suppress or we can create. Wealth and richness are innate in you, as well. You have ideas, talents, and resources that you haven't even begun to tap into. However, it is up to you to discover what lies dormant and put it to good (and profitable) use. Your belief system, your viewpoints, your attitude, and the discipline it takes not to look right or left but straight ahead will ultimately determine whether you just survive, or overcome and thrive. Your mind is your link to everything.

**“The process is agony,
but the victory is priceless.”**

"I SHOULDN'T BE HERE"
—ROBERT EVANS

I SHOULDN'T BE HERE. Experts have buried me for years, for decades. Artistically, commercially, financially, legally, and medically, at one time or another the best and the brightest have labeled me finished, washed up, broke, busted, and pushing up daisies. Yet here I am. I have survived in every way you can survive—I've survived marriages and divorces, blockbusters and flops, wealth and poverty, politics and business, fame and infamy, heartbreak and especially success, of every kind. None of them have killed me, though they gave it their best shot. Here I am. And not only am I not going under, I'm actively looking for more to do. Why? Because that's life—you have to live it to feel it. You have to push against time, you have to push against negative opinion, and you have to push against all odds to achieve something worthwhile in life. And when you do, you'd better be prepared to have it all taken away from you. So enjoy it while you have it. And then go enjoy some more.

I forget which wise man said, "Whom the gods wish to destroy they first grant all his wishes." Smart guy. Because I can tell you from my own experience that he was absolutely right. I was being kept by three showgirls by the time I was fifteen. I was a radio star before I was out of my teens. I was a success in business in my early twenties. I was tapped to be a movie star by Norma Shearer just hanging around the Beverly Hills Hotel pool when I was twenty-five. Though I was only a half-assed actor I learned what I really wanted to do while plying the trade—I wanted to produce. I wanted to be not the guy who parades around in front of the camera, I wanted to be the guy who decides who and what goes in front of the camera. I wanted to be behind the scenes. Before I was thirty-eight I got my first job in a movie studio—I was named head of Paramount.

Over the next fifteen years I put together or directly produced some of the most memorable films Hollywood has ever made. The partial list includes *Barefoot in the Park*, *The Odd Couple*, *True Grit*, *Harold and Maude*, *Rosemary's Baby*, *Love Story*, and *The Godfather*. As an independent producer I made *Chinatown*, *Marathon Man*, *Black Sunday*, *Urban Cowboy*, and *The Cotton Club*. I am the only producer listed on two of AFI's top five films of all time—*The Godfather* and *Chinatown*. I have received the key to New York City, a Lifetime Achievement Award from the American Film Institute, and I was appointed a professor at Brown University. Presidents and prime ministers, corporate chiefs and superstars, and movers and shakers of every kind have vied for my attention. And for years I couldn't get arrested, as they say. Few men have lived such extremes, even fewer have survived.

How did I do it? How did I survive attacks by the press, by corporations, and by the government? How did I come back from seven marriages? How did I overcome the infamy in a town that thrives on fame? How did I do it? And why?

From my earliest awareness, I knew that I was different. I hated being a follower of any kind. I was always trying to determine my own fate, and not let it be just something that happened to me. Or worse, to have it determined by others. I didn't want to be one of those people who spent their lives complaining about the things that "happened" to them. I understood early on what that was: a weak excuse for not pursuing your own dreams. And I had big dreams.

I learned quickly. Whenever I was thrown into a new situation—which happened a lot—I paid careful attention. I knew that to get what I wanted I would have to learn from the best, so whenever I was around someone who I believed knew more than me about something, I was careful to be as observant as I could possibly be. In almost any situation that you find yourself there's usually someone with more experience, more expertise, than you. Don't pretend to know more than you do. Pay attention. Learn. It's said that knowledge is power. I believe that this is true. In fact, I don't know any situations where this is not true.

Knowledge means different things at different times. Sometimes it requires technical expertise, sometimes it's psychological, sometimes it's artistic. Whatever it is, the knowledge that you bring to any given situation reflects what you have learned to that point. People who think that "expertise" is something confined to experts are not crediting their own experience enough. Sure, experts are necessary. But by their nature, experts tend to be narrow in their focus. If you can't afford to be narrow, if you have to have a broader view of something (like a producer), then you have to be aware of the limits of expertise and you have to be prepared to assert your own experience as valid and important. Otherwise, the experts will bury you.

A neurologist assured me that, after a massive stroke that I had suffered, I would probably never have anything like full mobility again, much less a full life. I told him to scram and I beat all his predictions, some of them by months. The process was agony, but the victory was priceless—not only over my own body, but over his "expertise." This has been a big part of the reason why I have survived. I've always lived my life publicly, so my problems and setbacks were well known. That meant that legions of people felt compelled (and empowered) to offer their opinions of me and my various life situations in public as well. As a result I was always aware of prevailing opinion. Especially when it was bad.

Other people feel that their world hinges on other peoples' opinions. I don't. When I would discover that people had said bad things about me or written bad things…I didn't care. In fact, just the contrary. I used it as motivation. I had known the heights of fame—Henry Kissinger interrupted détente talks with the Russians to attend the premiere of *The Godfather* at my request—and the depths of infamy—convicted in the court of public opinion of drug charges and being connected to murder—and in the end I've learned that you can't treat either one differently from the other. You shouldn't rest on your laurels any more than you should allow infamy or failure to keep you from trying again. A man is measured as much by his trials as his successes. Like Kipling said, "Treat those two impostors just the same." If I hadn't fallen so hard, I could never have come back so well. Everything that's happened to me has gotten me to this point, a point where I can look back with satisfaction at my triumphs, and with wisdom at my failures. Is that enlightenment? I honestly don't know…but it feels better than being dead. And when you've had a stroke and don't know if you'll ever be able to talk again, much less walk again—that's the fat lady doing her vocal exercises, if not actually hitting that final high E note. I've been there, I know a lot of people have been there, and I'm willing to bet that they've all learned the same thing I did: Life is better than death.

Once I accepted this seemingly simple fact, the rest was easy. I knew that to live well is the best goal you can have, so I determined to continue living well. For me that meant being active, not sitting back and waiting for life to come to me, but to take it back into my own hands. Once I did, and I felt the old magic of creation that I've always felt making movies, I knew that I had made the right decision. It's easy to lie down in the face of adversity. Most people do it at least once in their life. It's easy to feel like you're done, that you have nothing left. I don't have a monopoly on perseverance, I know, but I have picked myself up off so many floors and recovered so often from being left for dead that I can tell you from my experience—there is nothing so life-affirming as being mistaken for a corpse. When everyone writes you off, that's when you know it's time to get going.

And that's been the story of my life. Rocket start, rapid rise, crash, reinvention, fresh rockets. The fuel? The promise of magic. The promise of a new lease on life. Success rate? Not perfect, but enough so that I have good reason to keep anteing up. And I think that's the secret. We are not promised success, only the chance of it. No matter what your track record, as William Goldman said about Hollywood (but I think it can applied to life): No one knows anything. No one can predict with perfect certainty what the future will yield, or what one's chances are of achieving what you want. But the world rewards those who try, and generally ignores those who don't. Doesn't that simple fact seem to weigh in favor of trying again? It sure works for me.

There are too many examples of too many people overcoming too many calamities for me to be a pessimist. Pessimism is the weak answer to adversity. It's simple, it's comfortable, and it's cheap. And just like most things you can describe that way, it doesn't stand up to close scrutiny. When I think of how easy it would have been to fold up my tent…and when I think of the consequences, My God, how much time and effort has been wasted by pessimism.

When I was appointed head of Paramount, almost from the first day I heard that I was about to be fired, that the studio was about to be closed and sold for scrap. I had to fly to New York to deal with a couple dozen of the world's greatest non-smilers. I showed them a short film I had made by way of presentation—directed by Mike Nichols—in order to try to save my job (and the studio). I told these corporate bigwigs that I had an idea, I had a feeling, and I had a movie called *Love Story*. While I had them there I told them about another idea, another gut feeling I had, about a book called *The Godfather*. It would have been easy to skip that meeting, to accept the clods of earth hitting me (figuratively, of course) in the face. But if I had, who knows if those films, or any of the others I approved, would have gotten made?

Not everyone has the chance to do something they love, and to do it at the top of their profession. But everyone has the chance to try. Everyone has the chance to invest in their own dreams, in their own lives. Everyone has the chance to throw their adversity in the teeth of their destiny. Everyone has the chance to challenge their fates, good or bad, to another round. As one who has risen from many a canvas, I can tell you that nothing so affirms your life as the restating of it. Nothing can move you to renew yourself like your own faith in yourself. And even if there are no guarantees—and in this world, who can be certain of anything?—there is something more important than guarantees, more significant than "reasonable rates of return," more lasting than wealth and beauty and fame: there is hope. Not hope as in "I *hope* I can I *hope* I can I *hope* I can," but hope with teeth. Hope with the knowledge that you have worked and sweated to make something happen in the past…and it did. Sometimes to your shock and surprise, but happen it did. That experience alone should be bottled. Never forget that anything worth doing always began as someone's dream nurtured with hope to fruition. And that someone along the way told them they were crazy.

I'm crazy enough to believe that anything is possible. I started out selling women's clothing, never went to college, hobnobbed with kings and stars, and achieved my latest bout with fame as an animated cartoon. I have been married and divorced seven times and I'm still friendly with all my wives. I have walked it and talked it and I'm here to tell you that if it's crazy to dream, if it's crazy to hope, if it's crazy to keep trying, then color me nutty as a fruitcake, send for the butterfly nets, and ready the straitjacket, because that's me…and I won't go quietly.

"'You can' is not only a manifesto; it is a formula for empowering yourself."

WORDS THAT BUILD YOUR WORLD

In Genesis, we are told that God created the Earth by stating, "Let there be…. And there was." Then we are instructed in Job 22:28 to apply the same law of command in our own lives: "You shall decree a thing and it shall be established unto you and light shall shine upon your ways."

How do we decree a thing or command a thing? Words.

"Words are…the most powerful drug used by mankind," according to Rudyard Kipling. Gandhi understood and applied this knowledge when he stated, "Keep your thoughts positive because your thoughts become your words. Keep your words positive because your words become your behaviors. Keep your behaviors positive because your behaviors become your habits. Keep your habits positive because your habits become your values. Keep your values positive because your values become your destiny."

Are you living out your destiny? If the answer is "no" or "I don't know," then you have missed the fact that the law of command is the key to getting you there. We are constantly making decrees through our command of words. However, they are usually the wrong kinds of decrees and they usually manifest themselves as things that we do not want in our lives.

Students of the mind understand the true power of words—all words. Spiritual leaders throughout the world consistently teach their followers to speak only when something worthwhile needs to be said. Viewing idle words as counterproductive or dangerous, they know that a standard exists to determine whether something needs to be said or not. "Is it true? Is it kind? Is it needed?" If it is true but not kind, then it is not needed!

You can choose to take the high road or the low road in life. A mind that has been isolated by ignorance, stagnation, and poverty is the direct result of a lifetime of faulty thinking. Nothing short of constant and intense elevation into richer thoughts, attitudes, and expectations will turn the negatives into positives.

What is meant by this? Let's take a look at a few limiting words and how they affect our desired outcomes. The worst offender is often our use of the word *can't*. Stating that "I can't" sends the subconscious mind racing for supporting evidence. The mind will surely remind you of the reasons why you can't do whatever it is you are convinced you can't do… and you will be defeated before you even begin. The constant use of "I can't" will program your mental computer in such a way that you will continually perceive and experience limitation. Even when it is couched in a positive statement, like "I can't believe you were able to," the bias is revealed. "I can't begin to tell you…" actually does the opposite of what it says. "I can't understand how she can put up with…" when the truth is, you *can* understand it—all too well. "I can't" is a mental pause while your subconscious gathers its negative energies to confirm your certain knowledge that something really cannot happen, can't exist, or can't be understood.

When you are tempted to automatically spew out "I can't," stop and think what *exactly* it is that you mean. Do you mean that you don't want to? That it is too difficult? That it would take more time than you have right now? That you're not interested? Or could it mean that you simply never tried it before and are unsure if you're up to the challenge? But do you really mean that you *can't?*

In my own life it is a common joke that I have no sense of direction. "It's a missing gene," I blurt out at every opportunity. But do I really have no sense of direction? Or do I simply hate driving to unfamiliar destinations because I may take wrong turns and spend too much time in traffic, which makes my shoulders tense, and that may lead to a backache, and besides, I could be using that time to be doing more enjoyable things? Or perhaps I dislike having to focus on where I am going because I would rather listen to music, talk on the cell, or get lost in my thoughts while someone else does the driving? I could easily come up with dozens of legitimate reasons why it is a very bad idea for me to drive in an unfamiliar territory, and so I don't. But does this mean that "I can't"? How does that "can't" transform itself into limitations? We can count the ways: I can't control what the government does, I can't control what the weather does, I can't control what the prices are, I can't control the interest rate on my mortgage, I can't get a dream job, I can't have the love that I want…so why vote? Bingo! Half the electorate of the United States has come to this conclusion for many years. Why vote? Why bother? There is nothing I can do. By ceding control over the big things, like government, it is easier to give up control over the small things, like changing your environment, your relationships, and your life. "Can't" is one of the strongest limitations there is, a wall made of four letters that makes the Great Wall of China look like a sand castle on the beach. Even the obvious "cant's" can be overcome. No, you can't jump off the rim of the Grand Canyon and live, *without a parachute*. No, you can't fly to the moon, *unless you are NASA*. And no, you can't fight city hall, *unless you petition, sue, demonstrate, gain support, and win!* For every "can't" there is a powerful, and realistic, corollary that says the exact opposite. You can.

Another limiting word is *trying*. There's a saying that "trying is lying." Saying "I'll try" leaves a loophole big enough to march an army through. What is really being said when you say "I'll try" is, "Don't depend on me." But more than being an unreliable source for the recipient of your weak promise, you are telling your subconscious self that you are not a diligent and honorable person, that your word is not your bond. When you respond with "I'll try," you must ask yourself just what your real intention is. Will you try and give it your best, or will you try just to get that person or situation out of your face? Overusing "I'll try" subconsciously pulls you into the arena of failure. It is far smarter to say that you will not do what has been requested of you and disconnect your energy from that situation than it is to feign interest, do something halfway or not at all, and wind up in an energy drain. "I'll try" is first cousin to "I can't," but more cowardly. It says that "in spite of my best efforts, I may not be able to." It is tentative, weak, and gives you an excuse not to achieve whatever it is that's being asked of you. Did Kennedy say we would "try" to get the moon? Did MacArthur say he would "try" to return to the Philippines? Did Edison say he would "try" to invent the lightbulb? Not by a long shot.

Also included in the negativity hall of fame are "I should" and "I have to." *Should* and *have to*? Who is in charge of you? Who is pulling your strings? To what greater power are you responding? Where is your authority over yourself? "Should" and "have to" create an inner resistance that blocks a natural progress; they set up a subconscious internal rebellion. These words acknowledge that something you need to have done has not been done, but in reality they are usually used to give ourselves excuses for not doing them. "I should quit smoking" is the mental phrase that passes through almost every smoker's mind—right before they light up. "I have to pay my bills" is usually followed by the far more interesting activity of watching TV. Furthermore, telling yourself that you "should" or "have to" do something is in defiance of your inner authority values. Do you need an outside source to tell you what to do? This is the opposite of empowerment. This is self-limitation at its worst. This is imposing a wall on yourself that is not even necessary, much less representative of good judgment.

Next time you say "I should" or "I have to," ask yourself, "Do I want to do this or not?" Regardless of your reply, act accordingly. Clearly, you have to do things you don't want to, but then rephrase your response so as not to set up this defeatist mind-set. If you hate getting up early and driving two hours to work but you like the job and the money, say, "I choose to get up early and drive two hours to work because my career gives me great satisfaction." There is a wise way and a foolish way to proceed in life. The wise way expands our self-awareness and self-authority. The foolish way restricts our progress by creating roadblocks. Which category do you think "I should" and "I have to" belong to?

The perennial "I need" also seems unavoidable. Whether you're doing the talking or the listening, "I need" crops up sooner or later. What you really need is to change the negative. We think of needing to distance ourselves from a negative instead of going toward a positive, and we end up in negative territory every time. Even if you physically remove yourself from the negative situation, you most likely take it with you. As the old saying goes, "Wherever you go, there you are." If you constantly think about what you need less of instead of what greater thing you are moving toward, then that is what you will attract. This isn't a puzzle; it is very simple. For instance, if you require more shoes, do not say, "I need more shoes," but rather, "How can I get more shoes?" The statement takes the attention, and thus the energy, from a lack of something to the possibility of something. This statement redirects you away from what you don't have toward the means of getting something you require. "I need to lose weight" becomes "How can I lose eight pounds?"

As your words create your reality, they can be either productive or counterproductive. When you make false associations verbally, you justify things and create inaccurate manifestations of that thought process. In the end, it is the accuracy of your manifested reality that will attract positive outcomes. Not the desired manifestation—which, as we have seen, can be wrong—but the accurate manifestation; the true one. The truth can only set you free if you acknowledge what your own truth is and reject words that lead you to a false outcome. And make no mistake—the truth can set you free. But you must be willing to accept that freedom. You cannot resist the truth without doing grave damage to your reality. You will recognize the truth because it speaks to the deepest part of you, the part you have beaten down with "cant's" and "shoulds" and "have to's," until that part cannot do what is innate in every person—to transcend circumstance through the rational application of the truth. "You can" is not only a manifesto; it is a formula for empowering yourself.

Finally, I want to address the use and misuse of the most powerful and commanding words that we ever speak: *I AM*. Every single time you say, "I am," you affirm your reality and put out the energy that helps manifest this command. Whether you say, "I am not able to do this" or "I am not able to get this done on time," well, guess what? Neither statement deals with the problem before you. Focus! How often do you make thoughtless statements that create your reality and shape who you are? How often have you taken time and energy with these sorts of useless, energy-sapping words? With any negative "I am" statement, you are planning ahead of time what you will and will not be capable of doing, and you're informing others of the same. Not only do you then create your own negative energy but you also solicit others to do so on your behalf. It's bad enough that you are in the habit of limiting yourself, but do you really need anyone else's help? People fall into the same bad habits they have cultivated all their lives, yet the solution is available to everyone. And it starts with the words you choose.

Princess Diana was noted for saying, more than once, "I'm thick as a plank." How often do you say, "Oh, I could never do that"? What you are really doing is making it known that your level of incompetence has already been determined by the one who knows you best—you—so there is no need to assume otherwise. Furthermore, since you have drawn attention to this fact of your ignorance, it invites others to think about it as well and thus strengthen that affirmation with even greater energy. It is a self-replicating, life-crushing, endlessly repeated construct designed to steal your energy, waste your time, and prevent you from achieving. You know what acts like that in nature? Viruses and cancer.

All negative "I am" statements are to be avoided like asps. If you feel compelled to make one from time to time, defuse its power by making a supporting statement to yourself. For instance, if you say, "I feel exhausted," follow it by saying, "but I am feeling more energized with each passing minute and I will feel great by tonight." If you are compelled to acknowledge something that you cannot do for lack of time, but not for lack of desire, then say, "I will do it when I have the time, but that is not now." If you are convinced that someone is about to do something that will have a bad effect on him or her, when that person asks for your advice say, "You are perfectly free to act any way you want, but if you ask me for my opinion, I believe that this other action will give you the desired result without the certain detriment."

Often a lack of awareness is our greatest enemy. King Solomon warns in Proverbs 18:21, "Death and life are in the power of the tongue…and you shall eat the fruit thereof." James 3:5–6 gets more specific: "Even so the tongue is a little member, and boasts great things, behold, how great a matter a little fire kindles." He adds, "And the tongue is a fire, a world of iniquity; so is the tongue among our members, that it defiles the whole body, and sets on fire the course of nature."

The course of nature can be manifested in endless ways. It can be harmonious or chaotic, healing or destructive, happy or depressive. Our thoughts and words are the most powerful weapons we possess—they control the universal energy. Thus, as we mindfully choose our thoughts and words, which lead to our actions, we are creating our reality—and the reality of the world.

At the end of the day, thoughts, words, and actions of unconditional love, forgiveness, gratitude, and respect will only attract more of those things into our lives.

“I am now wise enough not to take too seriously the advice of people who have not been severely tested.”

"TREASURES OF DARKNESS" —JACQUELINE JAKES

WHO KNEW THAT ON an ordinary Monday morning in June my life would change forever? After collapsing on the job and being rushed to the hospital, for the next several months I began to have tests run to see what had happened and why I continued to feel so bad.

It was only my faith in God that kept my falling soul from a complete meltdown when I was diagnosed with a brain tumor. Five months after that fateful Monday morning, I was told to go to the hospital on November 11 for yet another test. I was also told that if I didn't pass this test that I would be scheduled for brain surgery, a craniotomy, the next morning, November 12, 1982. I didn't pass that test, and whatever happened in that eight-hour surgery took the next ten years out of my life.

On one of the many challenging days, I rehearsed the words of the doctors: "We didn't find a tumor but you had an A/V malformation. The arteries and veins were fused and intertwined, and we separated them. Your condition was something you were probably born with." The depression was smothering as I grappled with the challenges of trying to piece my life together and to find a place of ordinariness and normalcy again. Nothing and no one prepared me for such terror. I had no idea until this happened that life was so frail. I remember thinking many times that surely I would die. Surely no one could feel this depressed, this out of sorts, and not die. I descended into hell without leaving my chair. With no guidance for such a dark and frightening journey, I moved in silence against the alarming symptoms—seeing ghost lights on the side of my head where the surgery had taken place while listening to the strange chaotic sound of my little daughter's voice. I wandered aimlessly in the places of disconnect and yet I tried to appear like my normal self. I was nowhere near the person I had been before the surgery. I grieved enormously over the loss of my health, but I was determined to find my way back to health, to a place where I could recognize myself and feel at home in my own head and skin.

At twenty-nine years of age, quiet as a shadow, I groped into the next decade of darkness with a Bible in one hand and a strong will to raise my little girl in the other hand. What do you do when, without notice or an announcement, the bottom falls out of your life? One moment I had been at work, the next in a hospital. One moment I had been taking tests to see what was happening to me and the next moment I was sitting in a hospital bed with my head completely shaved and listening to the technician tell me that if I needed radiation for what was thought to be a tumor, it would be painless. I was raised a Christian and I did the only thing I knew to do: I renewed and clung to my faith in Jesus Christ. I panicked and ran deeply into the arms of a living, loving, and very real God.

I am amazed at people who do not know how suddenly life can change and how helpless you can become in the face of tumultuous times. It's still shocking to listen to and observe conversations that are totally void of understanding of how helpless we are without God. If He doesn't bless you, you can't catch your next breath. If He isn't merciful and faithful, you won't form your next thought. But I have to come to grips with the fact that only those people who have been tested beyond measure, and who have come face to face with the single most defining experience of their lives, could ever have the kind of wisdom necessary to know such things.

I am now wise enough not to take too seriously the advice of people who have not been severely tested. I garner information from people who will show me their wounds. I can usually tell from their testing whether the teaching is sound, whether to follow their advice, and whether it is wise to take their counsel. In the Scriptures, you will find a verse that says, everything that can be shaken, will be shaken, that the things which cannot be shaken may remain—Hebrews 12:27 (paraphrase). If you've not gone through a breaking or a life-shaking experience, learn from others who have. Don't teach anything yet. Observe the broken. Listen to the survivor. Study the life of the person who has surmounted the insurmountable.

For me, it was imperative to be the exception to the rule. I had to learn to never give up. I searched the Bible for people who had survived against the odds. I found them, and it refreshed my trembling soul to hear of Hezekiah, who had been told by the prophet Isaiah to prepare for death. But the Bible says that Hezekiah turned his face toward the wall and sought God's face for life, and he was given another fifteen years to live. I gained strength from his victory. If God helped Hezekiah, He would help me. And what about Naaman? Naaman was a leper and no one was ever healed of leprosy. No one but Naaman. My faith grew stronger. I memorized Scriptures to console and comfort my soul. I began to realize that someone else could have my hand, play it, and win. Why not me?

I will never forget standing at the foot of our staircase after tucking my little girl into bed. Everything was so hard and such a chore, but I tried with all of my might to keep my surreal experiences, depression, and trauma from my child. It had been several months after the surgery; our little house contained a spirit of forlornness. You couldn't have seen a more somber and sad environment. It was quiet and I was trying to find my way back to the person I had been before. I don't remember what was said that night, but I will always remember hearing the most shocking sound I had heard in months. Laughter escaped my lips. I didn't see it coming. I didn't even know that it was possible. The paint, the carpet, our little puppy, my child, our breathing, all stood still. I had laughed. It was such a strange sound. I turned it around in my mind. I melted into the sensation of what had just happened. Today, I know that no matter how mad and how low your life boils down, you will laugh again. It is inevitable.

What are you going through? Expect to win! Do you remember Nelson Mandela? How is it even remotely possible that a man could be incarcerated for 27 years, emerge from prison without hating those who had imprisoned him, and become the president of the country that had oppressed him and held him captive? How could Oprah Winfrey, born in poverty, rise to become a billionaire and the queen of TV?

God deals in impossibilities.

Through my quiet study of the Scriptures, time spent in prayer to God, listening and reading anything and everything that promised my healing and wholeness, I discovered that not everything sent your way should be signed for. What do I mean? I just received a package from UPS, and I checked to see if the package had my name on it. You should not receive those things that do not belong to you. My philosophy is that I will accept only what belongs to me. That illness wasn't mine. So I struggled to begin spiritual warfare for my health. In my mind, sickness didn't have a place in my reality. So I fought the good fight of faith to feel whole again.

Every Sunday my brother preached with fervor and fire, and no matter how out of sorts, how ill, or how sad I felt, I showed up for church. He wasn't the famous pastor, preacher, author, and successful entrepreneur that he is today, but he preached with the same passion and authority from the Scriptures. His ministry of God's word provided me with strength, and I sat at services writing notes from his sermons to carry back home to study for my personal comfort and the building up of my faith for the unexplored journey that lay ahead.

We are living in the most alarming times, and because we don't know what may come tomorrow, we have to grab hold of peace with all our might. How do you do that in the face of a battle? If I had known throughout all of my ordeals that I was going to ultimately come out and come out well, I would have lightened up. Yes. I would have relaxed more and worried less. I know you are probably in the midst of some trial that you think will never end, but if you will look to the end with a hopeful and positive attitude, you will fare better, no matter what. But you don't know these kinds of things until you have built up a résumé with trouble, until you are challenged to the limits. For me, worry magnified my depression and increased the overwhelming darkness. What I learned through this experience helps me today to remember to keep hope alive. You simply must look at your outcome and not the existing conditions. If you fixate on the smothering blackness, you won't see the way out; you won't receive the answers, the comfort, and the hope that is coming your way every second of the day.

Helen Keller once said, "If you stare at the door that has closed, you will not see the one that has opened." I try to find the open door. It's the same as when you are driving. You've heard the expression "a near miss." If you have ever narrowly escaped a car accident, you remember that you were caught up watching the debris roll in your direction, or the car come toward you, or the person step into the intersection. Rather than glancing to see if the next lane was free, or if there was an opening to avoid the accident, you stared blankly as an eyewitness to the event. Whenever that happens, I always look back and think, *Next time, I'm going to immediately look for the way out, and not get caught up in what is coming at me.* The same principle applies to trouble. You have to always look up and out to get the help you need. Keeping my mind solidly fixed on my Lord, the Savior Jesus Christ, remembering the Scriptures that promise me an expected and good end, and remembering that I am an overcomer, the head and not the tail, brings me comfort and ultimately the peace that I desire.

Not long ago I spoke for our Wednesday night Bible study at the Potter's House and talked about the "treasures of darkness." I learned about those treasures while going through my life and my situation. One of those Scriptures is found in Isaiah 45:1–3. Verse three reads: "And I will give you the treasures of darkness and hidden riches of secret places. . . ." For people going through the ordinary, mundane, and boring places of life, this verse will not be enlightening, but if you have some forbidding circumstances that you are facing, then you will see its implication and application to your life. I realize that this Scripture concerns Cyrus and Isaiah's prophecy to him about what he will find when he invades Babylon, but I saw something else. I saw these words as a personal promise to me, and indeed I did find treasures during my time of recovery. I found that when you are a believer in the Lord Jesus Christ, when you are in trouble, you might actually be in the *finest* moment of your life. I heard you gasp! But really, at my lowest point I had access to God in a way that I could never come close to now. Why? I told you earlier, "God is a very present help in the time of trouble." Most people can't touch God because they don't seek after Him with the urgency of a person who has been cast down to the "bottom of the mountains," a place of desolation described by Job. You don't pray the same, fast the same, or seek God's presence the same as does the sick, distraught, disfigured, and wounded soul. There is no comparison to the journey. There are things you will never, ever know about God when things always go well in your life. You can get help from God when you're in trouble that you could never, ever access on a sunny day. You don't need him in the same way. People who seek God are afflicted, and therefore focused and clear-minded. They are not distracted with shopping, sales, gossip, envy, or competitions. Life takes on more meaning. You become crystal-clear about the issues that are truly important in life. Your thoughts become focused on God's medicine for your soul—even if the issue is physical, you look for the root cause in the spiritual realm so that you can receive a permanent cure. You want wholeness, not just temporary help.

I used my faith in every way possible during my struggle. Funny, you don't know if you have faith until it is tested. You can quote Scriptures, practice principles, and everything else, but you won't know if what you believe is worthy or believable until it is tried by fire. My fiery trial was my difficult journey back into health.

You might remember the story of faith and trust that circulated on the Internet a few years back. It was called "Mountain Climber." The story goes something like this: There was a mountain climber with years of experience who set out one afternoon to conquer a mountain in Argentina. The man climbed for hours and to a high altitude when night fell thick, heavy, and black. That night there was no moon and the clouds covered the stars. As he neared the top, he slipped from a ridge and fell. As he fell through the blackness of night, his life passed before him and he was certain he would die. But he felt a powerful jolt around his waist that stopped his fall. He had remembered to stake himself with safety gear. The long rope tied to his waist held him tightly and he was suspended in the air. He began shouting, "Help me, God! Help me!" He later heard a heavenly voice asking him, "What do you want me to do?" Of course, he replied, "Save me!" The voice then said, "Cut the rope that is holding you up."

The rescue workers said that the next day they found the mountain climber suspended in air, frozen to death…*two feet off the ground.*

What would you have done? Do you trust God enough to follow His instructions? You see, we don't know if we trust God or have faith in Him until our faith is tried.

To know God's faithfulness and trustworthiness is a treasure usually found only in the turbulent times of our lives.

Sometimes I wish others could see a glimpse of me twenty-five years ago, returning home from an eleven-day stay in the hospital, staples in my head, moving slowly, hearing sounds, seeing the unfamiliar light on the right side of my head, feeling surreal, and trying to raise my sweet Kelly without any assistance. Then you would fully understand, and your faith would be strengthened because you would see how much of a miracle my life really is.

Time and time again, I have looked back over my life and realized how incredibly good God is. There are few things that I know for sure. One is: if God had not been on my side, pulling me out, rocking me out, kissing and comforting my soul, I would still be in a horrible condition. The other certainty is that if I had not had that horrific experience of recovering from the craniotomy, I would not be the person I am today. Who am I? I am someone who values life, who understands what is important, and who realizes that I am here for a reason. I have been marked by a bitter and savage experience, but sometimes God's best is temporarily bitter. That harsh and unpleasant place actually revealed that hope plus the fight of faith equals victory. And for me, once I received another chance at life, I never saw it the same way. Before, I wore life loosely, carelessly, and even disrespectfully. Now, I complain less, love more, and forgive more easily, and I've become more respectful of others, more compassionate, more clear, more grateful, and more determined than ever to live my life appreciating every good and wonderful second I am given. My eyes and my heart are wide open.

The psalmist David said, "It was good for me that I was afflicted." I don't believe he was into pain, but I think he knew that he became a better person in spite of and possibly because of his afflictions. One of my friends recently recounted a story that helps me with David's point. She said a reporter was assigned a story to interview a horticulturist who happened to have a showcase of plants and flowers worthy of note in the local newspaper. When the reporter arrived and began interviewing the gardener, he noticed that the man didn't seem to be excited about his plants. After a while, he came right out and asked him about his apparent dissatisfaction. The man quickly responded, "These plants need some drought." The reporter looked puzzled. The horticulturist continued, "I am concerned that these plants, which look so luscious and healthy, have not had enough drought. You see, because these plants have received so much rain, their roots are weak and flimsy. If they had experienced drought they would have had to dig their roots deep into the earth to find water, and that would have made their root system strong and healthy, but because they've not had to work through the dirt, they are weak in their root system, and when the strong rains and storms come, they will wash away."

I am glad for my drought—glad that it came and delighted that it went. It didn't make me perfect, but it made me recognize my weakness and my ability to survive the storms and struggles of life by placing my faith deep into the soil of God's love, grace, and mercy.

Now I am able to say it like Maya Angelou: "I wouldn't take nothing for my journey."

**“Like goods and services,
we can produce love deliberately,
usefully, and profitably.”**

THE POWER OF LOVE

Love is the essence of happiness. Our primary objective is to love and be loved. This desire is the source of the drive behind all of our actions, whether we realize it or not. Along with food and shelter, it is our greatest need. Yet how often do we not act with love toward ourselves or respond with love to others? How often do we fail to offer more than lip service to the idea of love? How many times have we let love be taken for granted?

Throughout our daily interactions, it is often a challenge to keep a loving presence about us. To act with love in our hearts can often feel like a perfunctory formula, rather than the empowering, energizing, and transforming power that it truly gives us. And yet, only love is the ultimate secret to success. You can master all the laws of prosperity and apply them with great diligence, but if you do not live harmoniously with others, if you do not practice love on an elemental level, then it is virtually valueless. Researchers have concluded that less than twenty percent of your financial success is due to your professional expertise. Thus, more than eighty percent of your capacity to prosper and thrive is due to your people skills. Your ability to be a conscientious, caring, considerate, and kind individual is therefore essential to succeeding. People may ask, Is it necessary for me to be loving to the postman I say hello to from time to time? Isn't that a waste of love? Is it necessary to constantly, consciously be acting with love in every moment? There are many levels of love. But love must inform your actions in all things. It may not always be conscious, but love can take many forms. It cannot be ignored. Some people call it impersonal goodwill, but whatever you label it—it is love in action. For all of your education, training, experience, and brainpower, unless you are able to get along with others, project a genuine caring for your fellow human beings, and know how to give and take fairly, your efforts—no matter how monumental—will be fruitless.

"Love never fails," according to 1 Corinthians 13:8. Jesus made it perfectly clear to the lawyer in Matthew 22:40 that love indeed fulfills the entire law—the law of a healthy, happy, harmonious, and prosperous life. If this is true, then it is necessary to be conscious of your love at all times. Love is a force so pervasive, so all-encompassing, that to be unaware of it is to be blind to the single greatest force at your disposal. Just as you can literally move mountains with love, so you can fail to lift your smallest finger without it.

Love is unequaled in its power. It has no rival because love is the power that unifies the entire universe and all within it. Love is the equalizing, harmonizing, balancing, and liberating force constantly at work in the whole world. When you connect with this energy, love will do for you what you could never do for yourself. It is necessary for us to produce all kinds of things in this world, from paper clips to laptops. But what people often forget is that love must also be produced. And like goods and services, we can produce love deliberately, usefully, and profitably.

Love is personal and impersonal. On a personal level, love is commitment, devotion, kindness, approval, and constant caring. On an impersonal level, love is about getting along with others and expressing goodwill toward them without personal attachment. Think about the people you meet. You automatically know who goes about just doing their job and who genuinely likes what they do and is conscientious about how they treat others. A good example is seen in doctors. It doesn't take a behavior expert to figure out who is in it for the money and who cares about their job and the people they are serving.

We can think of countless examples of how we felt and performed when love was present and when it was not. Two years ago, I was hit on the head with a golf ball on Christmas morning. At the time, I was on a tight book deadline. Upon my return from the hospital, my publisher called not to inquire about my well-being but to ask if I would complete the book on time. I met my deadline, but needless to say, there was very little love lost or generated with my publisher.

On the other hand, some years ago when a fellow author in London had a serious family crisis, he feared he wasn't going to make his deadline and was in danger of losing his book deal and the second half of a very large payment. He was beside himself and asked for help. I would get no credit, little money, and it would take some months of my time. I did the work, didn't take his money, and went my merry way. Nearly three years later, a high-flying political figure needed to have his autobiography ghostwritten. It was offered to this friend but he was already committed. Instead, he recommended me and I got the job. The book hit the top ten best-seller list in England and in many other countries. It ended up being the third-highest-grossing book of my career. In this case, a little love and lack of ego went a very long way indeed.

Life is a process of giving and receiving. Those of us who are not living in the stream of love suffer the consequences and feel its lack as difficulty in mind, body, and personal and professional success. When you consciously and deliberately do everything and encounter everyone with love, you will reap its rewards far in excess of what you ever expected. You don't have to look outward and hope that love will find you. By generating love from within toward others, it will come back to you multiplied.

Each day, observe how every word you speak or hear and every action you take or witness is either an expression of love or a cry for love. How simple it would be to respond to calls for love with love if we were only aware of this need. Once you become a loving presence to others, note the extraordinary changes that will take place in yourself. It never fails: acting from true love frees you to receive the love offered to you.

One of the more challenging aspects of becoming a loving individual is to learn how to carry your own atmosphere—you affect your environment instead of allowing your environment to affect you. Thus, when you come in contact with people who possess negative energy, let them be transformed by your good energy while not allowing yourself to be contaminated by their negativity. You must maintain a protective barrier around yourself while projecting a kind and considerate attitude. It is necessary to defend yourself from negativity, but not to the point of being blind to others' negative impulses. Be aware of them, but don't let them affect your spirit. This requires conscious effort, but it is conscious effort that pays for itself with enormous dividends.

Certainly, it is a challenge not to be affected by the competitiveness, one-upmanship, envy, jealousy, or any act of ill will from others. As my friend the late famed Hollywood supermanager Bernie Brillstein said—he even made it the title of his autobiography—"You're nobody until somebody wants you dead." The better the position you are in and the more successful you become, the more negativity will come your way. Successful people are often accused of "changing" when they "make it." But it has been noted, and I can attest to this, that it is not often the successful person who changes but rather how everyone around the successful person treats him or her. On the other hand, I also agree with Oprah, who has often stated, "If you are a nice person when you are struggling, you become a super nice person when you succeed, but if you are a jerk when you're down and out, you become a super jerk when you make it."

Therefore, you must practice being unaffected by the energy of others. You can be mutually productive and considerate toward their well-being but unaffected by their behavior. Bless those who don't wish the best for you; they may simply be lost in their own troubles, frustration, and anger. Your positive energy will cancel out their negative energy. This makes you a vulnerable target and you are more likely to experience the manifestation of *your* worries and fears. Let negative people become absorbed by their frustrations and anger. They don't have to be yours.

The greatest gift you can give yourself and others is love. When you think, speak, and act in a constructive and positive manner, you will experience an enduring sense of wholeness and inner peace. Only an ample supply of self-love will protect you from the constant bombardment of negative energy. A healthy love of self and compassion for others will permit you to deflect any potentially harmful energy. Jesus said that you must love others as much as you love yourself. This is a commandment to love yourself consistently and abundantly, and then to give it away. In this way is love renewed, your spiritual slate cleaned, and your energies marshaled for your own purposes. Getting deflected by another's unresolved issues, another's negativity, is the opposite of healthy self-love. It is buying into a downward spiral not of your own creation. Keep an eye on the negatives; they must be avoided at all costs.

Without doubt the greatest power that love has is the power of renewal. Love given freely recharges itself, re-creates itself, and reinforces itself. It is the one thing that, if given generously, returns to you redoubled and tripled. And that is the essence of love: It is the gift that keeps on giving, to the recipient and to the giver. Love does not ask for returns; love is not a shrewd investment plan. That's the point: love must be given freely *in order to be* love.

If "love" is given as a way of incurring a debt, it is not love. If love is given as repayment of an alleged debt, it is not love. If love is given with a thought to how it will influence another person's feelings or thoughts about you, it is not love. If love is given as a cudgel to hold over someone else, it is not love. If you love from obligation, you do not love. If you love because it is financially beneficial to you, you do not love. If you love because you fear the results of not loving, you do not love.

Love is freedom, love is generosity, love is finally and completely unselfish. That does not mean that love is blind or foolish. Love is clear-eyed. Love is being able to see people for who they are and knowing the difference between those who are worthy of your love and those on whom it is largely wasted—and giving it anyway. Love requires no receipts. It is the feeling of absolute giving, and so it has the result of being absolutely replenishing. Love is discerning, love is insightful, and best of all, love reveals true character.

Who do you love? Why? How often do we stop and ask ourselves these questions? Not often enough. Love is thought by many of us to occupy some box in our brains, a box we can open and rummage through whenever we need it, or are obligated to it, or remember it. But true love is not a commodity that you can put on tap. It is not something simply available when you want it. It must be renewed and questioned and affirmed, over and over. It can't be something you are unwilling to risk; it must be something you are ready to assert. I love, therefore I am! By exercising your true power of love, you can free yourself from the traps of the past, the traps that keep you from feeling the greatest emotion known to man. By exercising your true love you can find sources of strength that you thought exhausted, sources of inspiration you thought dried up, and sources of creativity you didn't know you had.

Exercising the power of love is a constant effort, but one that renews itself every time. By loving others truly, it becomes possible not only to see them clearly but also to see yourself clearly. If you are miserable and depressed and sure that you cannot continue, that is when you must test yourself to see if you have properly assessed your life. This must begin with love. Have you loved yourself enough? Have you loved yourself properly? Have you given credit where credit was truly due? Or have you selfishly pitied yourself and not truly explored the reasons for your predicament? A loving, clear-eyed analysis of who you are and what you care about and what you want and what you love should shake out the cobwebs, clear the decks, and brace you for what you have to do. Any other kind of analysis, any analysis that does not take love into account, is not worth the time wasted on it.

It is in the worst moments of crises that love shows its true importance. When you have been beaten, or believe you have been beaten in life, that is when you need love the most. Have you prepared your love for these moments? Have you just taken it for granted? Love must be nurtured, grown, cared for, and developed in all its infinite possibilities. Love will not be ready for you if you haven't prepared the way for it. Because when you are down and out, when you think you've hit rock bottom, that is when love's greatest strength can save you. Love will allow you to change, to adapt, to overcome, and to triumph over the most bitter despair. Love will give you the strength to hold on to yourself just as you are in the process of transforming that self into something you might not ever have considered possible. Love will allow you to become a new person even as you retain the integrity of your character and personality. Love is change at its best—for the better. Consider all the times you thought you were without love, either given or received. Were you really receptive to love? Were you able show love at those times? Was love something you worked on? Or was it just something you expected?

The transforming power of love is something that is shown to us all the time if we care to notice it. How often do we pay close attention to the renewal of springtime? Every year change is demonstrated in the nature that we so often try to ignore or control. Earth herself shows us with every season that the hope of life in the future is a hope of transformation, of transcending the old and giving way to the new. And yet we ignore this devastatingly simple and powerful message all the time. Love is clear-eyed because it must confront tragedy and transformation; it risks itself constantly in its generous desire to help others, regardless of the cost. Love creates change because in its essence it is fearless.

Knowing its own power, love will come out when it is needed. But if we know its power, and we know that we can produce it, why don't we have it available to us at all times, and not just when it's needed? Why do we consistently ignore the one thing that we all know is the answer to every problem? Because we mistrust ourselves, our feelings, our thoughts, and our plans. What CEO will call a meeting to emphasize the importance of love? What manager will talk about love as the key to the big game? And yet, we all know the truth: love is the answer.

“Health can’t be achieved without joy.”

"HOW TO CHANGE THE WORLD"
—Dr. Patch Adams

I've achieved a certain fame as a doctor and a clown, not necessarily in that order. I have traveled all over the world bringing an idea of health to people. That's been an important mission for me, because I'm not just a traveling doctor. There are plenty of those, and they do wonderful work. No, my job is not only to cure the sick, but also to make them healthy. This is not easy, since sick people, once they are cured, usually return to the patterns that landed them in sickness. My job is to show them a different way of looking at their health. It is not just about pathology and recovery. To live a healthy life takes a conscious commitment. If you stop trying to live a healthy life, if you become consumed by the stresses of your life, then you have to overcome a lifetime of conditioning to get healthy. And I am here to tell you that a lifetime of conditioning is not an easy thing to overturn. Try being a six-foot-four-inch clown sometime to get a taste of what I mean.

I was raised overseas in a military family. My mother was from the Old South, and after my father's sudden death when I was sixteen she became the source of all my love and support. She believed in manners and appearances, to the point where it was hard to discuss things that were upsetting or difficult. This gave me an intense curiosity in the things that could be discussed, like math and science. I was very good at both, and this meant that from an early age my mind was free to wander in class. I was bored, as many bright students are, by the things in school that didn't interest me. I learned to be a clown to get over being bored. It just carried over into my adult life to a degree that's not…usual.

In medical school I worked several months in a Washington, D.C., hospital, and I was determined to bring some joy to the lives of the patients there. It was a pediatric ward, so the need for comic relief was obvious. It also helped that I had friends, fellow residents and doctors, who supported my "antics." I will never forget the joy of those children. It has helped sustain my passion for what I do. Nothing that anyone thought about me, and certainly nothing that anyone ever said about me or to me could possibly compare with a single smile from a sick child who had felt better but for my antics. It was a valuable lesson to learn. I've carried it with me.

People lead lives of quiet desperation, it is said. I've certainly seen that this is true. But however desperately they live their lives, people are still in need of compassion and love. Compassion and love! Lives lived fully are full of them, lives lived without them are inevitably sad, and ultimately unhealthy. I have found that some of the most effective treatments for illness are extra-generous helpings of attention, listening, care, and compassion. Empathy is often worth more than all the advanced medical technology can hope to provide. The simple reflection of another's pain is a powerful medicine. It's not taught in medical school, where they are busy with drugs and machines and treatments designed to attack pathology. They have their work cut out for them. I see my role as not just curing illness but also promoting health. Health can't be achieved without joy. Yes, people can have excellent blood pressure, great strength, terrific cholesterol numbers, a heartbeat like a metronome, perfect balance in the blood gases, tiny prostates, a full head of hair, dazzling smiles…and be perfectly miserable. There are a million reasons for this, but the one I always see in lives blighted this way is the absence of joy. How do you achieve joy? That journey is different for everyone, but my advice about it is this: If you are lucky enough to find something in life that brings you joy, hang on to it with both hands, all your fingers and toes, and all the strength of your heart. Nurture it, promote it, share it, spread it around everywhere you go, because there is only one way to be truly joyful, and that is in sharing something you find important. If you do this properly, I've found that this joy renews itself every time. Don't hoard anything! Anything worth having is twice as valuable if you give it away.

I've seen this work. I've seen passion and persistence change lives, and I believe passion and persistence can change the world. Has anything else ever changed the world? Passion and persistence should not be astonishing, or even remarkable. I dream of a day when they are the norm, when being a crusader for a cause is not weird, but common. Passion and persistence can be inspired, studied, desired, and pursued, but they cannot be taught. They must be felt. I consider myself a designed person. Everything I do has an intention. This is the result of having consciously confronted life every chance I got. I have believed in myself when others did not. I have hung in there against opposition, indifference, and outright rejection. Did they stop me? No! Did they make me more determined? Yes, but not as much as the simple confidence I felt when I knew I could make people feel better.

People overlook their own potential more than they realize, and certainly more than is healthy. They overlook the positive effects they have on others, or the positive effects they could have on others. They are prepared to accept the word of experts, words like *critical*, *radical*, *surgery*, and *phases*. They have a powerful effect, and people accept them unquestioningly. But how many examples of patients defying the odds to recover from "mortal" illnesses and accidents will it take before people understand that "experts" aren't always right? That experts have their own agendas, which have more to do with proving their own self-image than curing illness? How many times must we hear of a "miracle" cure before we draw the conclusion that there must be medicine and treatments that don't require a lot of scary words to be effective?

I wish I knew. But I can tell you there is nothing miraculous about love. Love and its companions, compassion and empathy, have overcome mortality more than once. It seems incredible that more people are not more willing to examine their beliefs in light of this, yet they aren't. The doctors, the HMOs, the insurance companies, and the pharmaceutical companies have their hooks in deep. They have managed, alone and in concert, to both terrify and anesthetize us. We are afraid of getting sick, going to hospitals, taking drugs, and recovering. We have been taught to fear everything, from tap water to cell phone radiation. The result of all this fear-mongering is a widespread willingness to medicate our problems away. We now have drugs that "help" us pay attention, relax, wake up, go to sleep, get erections, have babies, and not have babies. Those are just a fraction of a percentage of the things we now take drugs for. Where is the pill for love? Wait for it, because there is certainly a shrewd advertising agency pushing a pharmaceutical client to develop such a thing. Think of the profit margins if you could market pure love! Alas, they can try all they want. Some things can't be manufactured, packaged, and sold. Some things you have to come by the old-fashioned way. Love may be the best example. Maybe that's why it comes so hard to people. They keep expecting to trip over it, like a rake left in the driveway. But that's not the way to have love in your life. Love is a promise made and kept. It is a condition that you feel, but also one you can create. One thing about it is certain: no one does well without it. It is also different for everyone; no person experiences love the same way as another. That means we have to tolerate it, welcome it, and learn all about it when we experience it. Once you have experienced true love you should feel free, not trapped. Love is not an obligation that implies ownership; it is a liberation that inspires joy. Exploring and developing life should be the real goal of everyone. But too many feel stopped, thwarted, and cheated out of their love. Cynicism and apathy around them confirm their worst fears—that there is no such thing as love. To compensate for having been deprived of this source of life, people retreat into their psyches, nursing wounds that may not immediately manifest as illness, but which contribute to illness, exacerbate illness, and ultimately cause illness.

Fighting this has been my life's work. Once I understood that hopelessness was something shared by nearly everyone, I got to work. I am an extreme extrovert, so for me this meant dressing up and clowning. But this source of passion is different for everyone. Quiet people pursue lives of great dedication in just as passionate a way as I ever have. You don't have to put a rubber ball on your nose and make children laugh to be passionate about what you do and to persist in doing it against all odds. The trick is to pursue that passion with joy. Enjoy what you have achieved! No one else has done it quite the way you could, if at all! Treasure the moments of success and use them to reinforce your beliefs and convictions. They should serve you as proof that, yes, you too can make a difference in another person's life. Aren't there plenty of doomsayers and doubters? Do we need any more? And aren't all those people just looking for someone to inspire them? Don't they secretly want to change, to believe, to participate? Don't they want a good reason to stop complaining? I have been trying to promote health in this way for many years. With the help of many friends of mine, I have been trying to build a hospital on these principles. We have the land, the plans, and the commitment of an unbelievable number of enormously dedicated people. But a nontraditional hospital is not an easy concept to sell. People expect hospitals that are white, cold, forbidding places. Recovery should be painful and difficult, not funny. Overcoming illness should be a grave, grim affair, not a laugh a minute. You should lift weights to recover, not garden to recover. There should be no clown classes in hospitals!

Sorry. I've grown used to the no's. They are like rain now—a natural phenomenon, nothing more. When so many people say, "No, that's impossible" to something that you *know* is not only possible, but necessary, it should be a clue that you are on the right path. What great idea was ever met with anything other than scorn? This has been a key to my persistence. Since I am passionate about what I do, believe in it so much, and see it have so many wonderful results, I know that my persistence is warranted. I have never doubted it the way so many people doubt the paths of their lives. If properly implemented, passion and persistence can lead to joy and love. Joy and love, in turn, fuel the passion and persistence necessary to overcome the speed bumps that people put in their own paths.

I've been lucky. But I've worked at it. It wasn't easy, though I made sure it was fun. I had to overcome prejudices, locked-up mind-sets, tradition, institutional orthodoxy, and "experts," but I was sure of what I was doing, so I did it. People responded, as people will when you are sincerely trying to share something valuable with them. They have helped me confirm my ideas, to myself and to many others. They have taught me at least as much as anything I've ever done for them. By trusting in them, by honestly sharing with them, by working to help them, I have received tenfold anything I've ever given.

I am filled with joy for the adventures of the future. I have love to guide and carry me. I work hard at what I do and it has repaid me more than I could ever have anticipated. Isn't that a good reason to keep looking? I'm not done with my exploration of life. Are you?

“Victims choose stagnation and pain; victors choose peace and prosperity.”

THE LIBERATING POWER OF FORGIVENESS

NOT TO FORGIVE IS TO be imprisoned by the past. Like Lot's wife, living in the past turns us into metaphorical pillars of salt; it paralyzes us and prevents us from going onward on our life's journey. We are known to lug along our hurts and grudges for years or decades, and sometimes we even hand them down to the next generation. Often we repress such hurts from conscious memory and do ourselves far more harm than those whom we would rather take revenge on. We simply don't realize how self-destructive an unforgiving spirit can be.

Doctors and therapists have long known just how much damage can be done when we fail to forgive. As I stated earlier, the medical community has overwhelmingly stated that the majority of our illnesses are caused by emotional factors like resentment, which can stem from a lack of forgiveness. The roots of bitterness can easily be seen in depression, anxiety, and toxic relationships. Old grievances simply do not permit our lives to proceed with new matters.

When we choose not to forgive, we are not punishing the other person but rather yielding to another's control. If you do not forgive, then you are controlled by the other person's initiatives—you are in step with action and response, outrage and revenge, and thus constantly fueling the fire and spreading the damage. Your present is forever consumed and devoured by the past.

There are many myths about forgiveness. Chief among them is that we are to "forgive and forget." To the uninformed, this translates as: stop talking about it; stop complaining; let the offender off the hook; just be quiet and get on with it. Or, as someone once advised me after I had been professionally ripped off, "Suck it up!" Let me tell you, that was the last thing I was about to do!

Most of us wish to forgive because experience has taught us that forgiving feels better and is smarter than hurting and hating. We want to be generous and compassionate and not wish anyone ill will, and yet it seems such a difficult thing to do when we are wronged.

So let's begin at the beginning: to forgive does not mean to forget. To forgive does not mean that you are a greater person, a martyr of any kind, or that your trust is automatically renewed and that reconciliation is at hand. Once you forgive, it's no longer business-as-usual, where you continue to be offended or taken advantage of. You can forgive and still submit the invoice, reinforce the court order, or file the lawsuit.

Many people believe that in order to forgive someone, first they must come to us with an apology. Of course, an apology, contrition, reparations, and some convincing gesture of sincerity that it was a mistake, a temporary lapse of sanity on their part, and the swearing that it will never happen again would make it much easier for us to accept the apology, forgive, and move on. Not only should an apology be offered up, it should be done speedily.

Not quite. Not in the real world. Forgiveness should not have strings attached; it is not a bargaining chip or a means to manipulate someone who has wronged us. Why risk our desire to forgive—and free ourselves—by putting the outcome in their hands?

Of course, many of us want to forgive but feel that it would be letting the offender get away with it. Forgiveness and justice are not bedfellows. You are free to forgive and still do the right thing. I forgave a dentist who royally screwed up my teeth, but I still filed a complaint with the Board of Dental Examiners, who reviewed the case and voted to have his license revoked. This was not revenge; it was sparing other people from suffering at the hands of an incompetent dentist.

Still, there are those among us who believe that forgiving implies that the offense was somehow justified. But to forgive is not to condone. An offense is not overlooked, minimized, or trivialized when it is forgiven, but just the opposite—it is significant enough to warrant forgiveness. When a trusted member of our household staff was repeatedly caught stealing and bringing unauthorized persons into our home while we were away, he was forgiven. However, he was fired. We have no desire or intention to punish him further, but he is no longer allowed on the premises. If we held on to ill will, we would in essence be allowing him to violate us over and over again.

If enough time has passed, many of us may feel that we somehow have automatically forgiven an offender. Not so. We're fooling ourselves into thinking that we have forgiven someone when in reality we have not. One of my friends, who had ended a verbally abusive relationship, was certain that she had forgiven him as several years had passed since they had been in contact. When they unexpectedly came face-to-face in a business meeting, she was as cool as a cucumber, and he felt assured that what had happened between them wasn't that bad. After all, she chose to leapfrog through the process, bypass any conflict, avoid the consequences, and arrive at a neutral, if not happy, place in her current situation. But as we all know, you can't go from the freezer into the frying pan, and pretending that you forgive someone when you simply choose to bury it is not forgiveness at all.

Forgiveness is a choice. We forgive by faith because forgiving goes against our nature—it does not come easily for most of us. Our instinct wants us to recoil in self-protection when we have been wronged. We don't naturally overflow with mercy and grace when we have been hurt. But God instructs to forgive first and foremost. Colossians 3:13 says, "Bear with each other and forgive whatever grievances you may have against one another. Forgive as the Lord forgave you."

The fact remains that forgiveness is empowering. I recently had dinner in New York with my old friend Dennis Kneale from *Forbes*. He appeared pensive and a bit distracted. Finally he posed the question: "Jules, would you rather forgive or be forgiven?" Without missing a beat, I replied, "Forgive, of course!" But he wasn't buying it. He was pondering this seemingly weighty issue and it was causing him a considerable amount of visible grief. "Wouldn't you want the burden of nonforgiveness lifted from you?" he pursued. After thinking what on earth he might have done, I stuck to my guns. "Dennis, is your contentment and happiness dependent upon the behavior of someone else?"

He insisted that I wasn't getting it. I began to wonder if he wasn't just wallowing in some useless guilt. The only function of guilt is to prevent you from taking some action. It's a form of martyrdom. Guilt robs you of your power and turns you into a victim; it's misplaced energy aimed at rendering you weak.

My accomplished and compassionate friend is anything but a victim, yet from time to time we all wrestle with the issue of forgiveness—whether we require it or need to offer it. But no bravery is required to be a victim. There are those among us who are so accustomed to chronic pain—whether emotional, spiritual, or physical—that on some level, we are constantly seeking to re-create it. Victims choose stagnation and pain; victors choose peace and prosperity.

It has been noted that forgiveness is a journey toward freedom from our past; it is a gift we give ourselves. By forgiving the people who have hurt us, we free ourselves from the chains of resentment and other destructive thoughts that have occupied our hearts, minds, and bodies. When you forgive, you take away any control the offender has over you. It is an act of ultimate self-empowerment and freedom. It is a liberating force that will start you on the path of growth and prosperity. To truly forgive is to have weight fall off, to be newly energized, to finally see the way forward.

The process of forgiveness is transformational; it is thoughtful and complex, and it cannot be accomplished on command. The road to forgiveness requires time and consciousness. How will you know if you have truly forgiven? You will know when all the emotion that you have felt for the offender is replaced with only love and gratitude. Don't be fooled, however. A generic "sorry" that you accept because that's the expected thing to do does not mean that forgiveness has been genuinely offered or accepted. If no effort has been made to understand or learn from the situation, then the hollow "sorry" has no value at all.

Again, forgiveness is the ultimate liberator from our past. It means that you have done the difficult work of unmasking emotions and confronting unfinished business. You have processed it and gained knowledge and wisdom from it. You have released all negativity and now you have taken your power back. Whatever issue or situation has kept you in emotional bondage has been broken to pieces, and you are no longer feeding it with your energy. You choose the right to be free. You no longer identify yourself with the event. But you do learn from it, and you can now help others who may be stuck there.

Forgiveness is possible because we have the power to make choices. When we choose to forgive, no one can prevent us from doing so, no matter how vile the offense may have been.

This evolved maturity and wisdom that lets us forgive indicates the control we have over our lives. But how much more control would we have over our lives if we chose not to be offended in the first place? As if forgiving someone who has caused grief and harm is not challenging enough, imagine possessing the inner resources that would make it virtually impossible for anyone to offend you, intentionally or otherwise, in the first place. Imagine exercising your power of choice to limit the number of instances in which you are offended so that the need to forgive rarely arises. Choosing to live your life in a manner that deflects offense and increases compassionate understanding is the ultimate enlightened path to peace and prosperity.

Elisabeth Kübler-Ross identified denial, anger, bargaining, depression, and acceptance as the five stages of grieving. When acceptance fails, you forgive. When a relationship ends, a dream is not fulfilled—you suffer a disability or a blow to your self-esteem and you feel empty and bitter within the core of your being. You begin by forgiving. You forgive the one who left you, the one who offended you simply because the person filled *that* space. Forgiveness completes the grieving process and allows you to go forward, to become stronger, wiser, more loving, and more prosperous. When you function with an open heart instead of a clenched fist, the world and everything in it belong to you.

After all, a person who cannot forgive cannot dream.

"I'm not ending up—
just beginning again."

"THE ETERNAL HOPE FOR REDEMPTION" —JUDGE SOL WACHTLER

I WAS ONCE KNOWN for my historically significant landmark decisions on civil rights for women and the handicapped, free speech, the right to die, and for banning discrimination. I was New York Chief Judge Sol Wachtler. I rose to the top of my profession and was a major figure in New York politics, considered an odds-on favorite to be New York's next governor. But in November 1992, in a matter of months, the career of this rising judicial star was erased in a whirlwind of scandal over an affair that led to my imprisonment for harassment. Diagnosed as suffering from bipolar disorder exacerbated by self-medication, I resigned my judgeship, resigned from the New York Bar, and spent thirteen months in a federal prison's mental health unit.

Although no life is free of transgression, the major transgression in my life virtually invites condemnation. Fifteen years ago, I engaged in a bizarre pattern of behavior involving the harassment of a woman with whom I had an ongoing relationship. I confessed my transgression, resigned from the judiciary, which had been a part of my life for twenty-five years, and served a year incarcerated in federal mental health facilities. By my conduct, I ruined a long career in public service and forever tarnished a legacy that I would and should have left to my children and grandchildren.

I suffer from bipolar disorder, which I now control with medication. I am ashamed to say that because of the stigmatization of mental illness, I did not avail myself of the psychiatric help I needed—the help that my wife, Joan, a trained and licensed social worker, urged me to seek. I was afraid that if my seeing a psychiatrist became public knowledge, it would ruin my chances of becoming governor. It was my own narcissism and ambition that kept me from seeking help—that, and not my mental illness, was my true weakness. Had I sought the help I needed, I am certain I would not have brought shame to my court, my profession, and myself.

When I was in prison, one of my fellow inmates, a former FBI agent, asked me the rhetorical question, "Whoever thought we would end up like this?" If I were able to answer him today, I would say, "I'm not ending up—just beginning again."

I begin by knowing more about a world I had dealt with all my adult life but never saw; more about mental illness and its stigma; more about mortal weakness and the frailty of the human spirit, and how little we understand those we condemn. I have learned a great deal more about myself.

I have also learned the importance of friends and family, those who are unflinching in their devotion and attention. Every person who is in a position of significance should fall from grace just long enough to sort the wheat of true friendship from the chaff of opportunistic association. These friends and my family encouraged and convinced me that I am capable of living a good and productive life.

Of course, my first thought on leaving prison was to consider retiring to Santa Fe, New Mexico. Spending the last years of my life in anonymity was very tempting. However, I was mindful of the love and devotion of my wife and children, as well as my friends, which never diminished. It was far more than I deserved and it was their encouragement that brought me to a firm resolve: I would do what I could to attempt—in some small way—to seek redemption and to justify their love. I also resolved to put to use those lessons I learned during a life filled with exaltation and degradation—lessons learned from living with the law and the lawless.

But how? I was sixty-four years old, had no license to practice law, and had no business or profession waiting for me. I had no job.

A few years before my fall, a taped recording of a speech I delivered before an audience of over 5,000 people at the Chautauqua Institution sold more copies than any other of their presentations that summer. There was a time when I was invited to speak before bar associations and other groups all over the country. I once delivered twelve addresses in one week in four states. Over my twenty-five years as a judge I had garnered thirteen honorary degrees. Over a four-year span, the United States Information Agency sent me to seven European countries as a speaker on the United States Constitution.

But now, still bearing the wounds of my disgrace, and although I had so much more to say, no one seemed interested in hearing me.

"With my background, I can do one of two things: teach law or become mayor of Washington, D.C."

"Thank you for telling me how good I look. Your compliment reminds me of the story of John Wesley Hardin. After a lifetime of inflicting physical violence as an outlaw, he was gunned down by a longtime sworn enemy. The next day's territorial newspaper carried his obituary, quoting the coroner, who said, 'If it weren't for the fact that Mr. Hardin is dead, he would be in excellent physical condition.'"

Icebreakers, they are called. Those are the opening lines of the speeches I was prepared to deliver. It would be a lighthearted way of acknowledging my imprisonment and letting my audience know that I was aware of my demise.

The only trouble is, I received very few invitations to speak. Those invitations I did receive, I believe, were those who wanted to see what "had happened" to me. I had the same attraction as a train wreck.

I was always told that I was a good teacher and so that seemed a vocation to pursue. After all, I had learned and written the law for more than a quarter of a century. In addition to having been privileged to serve as New York's chief judge, I had been chair of New York's Free Press/Fair Trial Committee, and chairman of New York's Constitutional Bicentennial Commission. The dean of Fordham Law School, where I had delivered a commencement address and several discourses, once told me that I was one of the most talented lecturers he had ever heard. He went so far as to tell me that if I ever wanted to teach, I would always be welcome at his law school. Of course, when he engaged in that flattery and extended that invitation he had no way of knowing that he was speaking to a soon-to-be convict. I tried twice to reach him by phone after my release from prison. He returned neither call.

I wanted so much to become part of academia, not only because I thought I would do well at teaching law but also because I thought it was a wonderful way to redeem myself.

For a while I thought that redemption was at hand. When I was in prison, Jay C. Carlisle, a law professor at Pace Law School, wrote to me on a regular basis. His letters were addressed to "Chief Judge Wachtler" and were welcome reminders of the world I had left behind. We had met and corresponded when I was still a judge. I was familiar with his legal writings and excellent reputation as a scholar, but we had no association beyond that.

In a series of letters shortly before my release, he urged me to consider teaching law at Pace. He told me that those responsible for making faculty appointments were pleased with the prospect. This idea excited me. I had been associated with the law school at Pace since its inception, had launched its law review, and was the recipient of one of its honorary doctoral degrees. I was the law school commencement speaker in 1992, and Professor Carlisle's invitation brought back memories of a congenial faculty and a bright, receptive student body.

Permission was given for me to leave the halfway house for an afternoon so that I could deliver a lecture to one of Professor Carlisle's classes. I considered it a sort of audition. The experience was exhilarating. Professor Carlisle wrote me telling of the enthusiasm of the class and that he felt he had "learned more than the students."

The newly installed dean of the law school indicated that Pace would be pleased to have me teach, but that because of the timing, it would be impossible for my position to be included in the budget for the current year. I told him that I was not interested in being paid. Being given the opportunity to return to the law—to teach the law I had helped write—would be compensation enough.

My assignment was to teach alternate classes in New York practice with Professor Carlisle. "Team teaching," it is called. It was to be, as the professor wrote me, "the best New York practice course in the history of the Empire State!" And it started off that way. The class was well-attended, its complement of close to 100 senior law students attentive, excited, and exciting. Because I had written many of the opinions in the text and had been on the Court of Appeals when almost all of the others were written, I was able to share with the members of the class elements and insights of the court's reasoning not readily apparent from merely reading the court's decision.

Perhaps there could be a life for me after all; the redemption I hoped for might be at hand.

And then, after some six weeks, Professor Carlisle told me that he had been advised that my services were no longer wanted, that complaints had been received, not about my teaching—which he assured me was "fantastic"—but because there was fear of "criticism" if I were permitted to continue. He asked me to return one more time to say good-bye to the students. I did, telling the students that the only person to be blamed for my unacceptability was me. That I had, by my conduct, forfeited the right to be judged in the same way as others should be judged.

I received many letters from students who were in my classes expressing their gratitude and regret; one even told me, hyperbole I am sure, that he had learned more in that class than he had "during the rest of his law school career." But I never heard from the dean, neither to apologize for the indignity of being "fired" nor to thank me for my efforts.

Of all the undertakings that have absorbed my energy and commitment, the one I have found the most redemptive and gratifying has been the work I have been doing with the mentally ill and the stigma of mental illness.

As a member of the executive committee of the North Shore-Long Island Jewish Health System, I felt something should be done. I also felt that, having had strong ties to the judicial branch of government, and having felt the sting of the treatment inflicted on the mentally ill in prison, I was in a unique position to do something.

In 1841 Dorothea Dix discovered that the mentally ill were being confined in this nation's prisons. She began a nationwide crusade to remove these persons from prison—to see to it that they were put in treatment facilities. Speaking before the Massachusetts legislature she said:

> "I proceed, Gentlemen, briefly to call your attention to the present state of the Insane Persons confined within this Commonwealth, in cages, stalls,

> pens! Chained, naked, beaten with rods, and lashed into obedience."

As a result of her crusade, states created psychiatric hospital systems, and the number of severely mentally ill prisoners nationwide was reduced to less than one percent.

Since 1970, ninety percent of these psychiatric hospitals have been closed and the mentally ill are again being put into our prisons. Today, there are more than 350,000 seriously mentally ill prisoners behind bars: sixteen percent of our jail and prison populations. We have transinstitutionalized these prisoners from the psychiatric hospitals into the cells. It has reached the point where law enforcement personnel, corrections officers, and the criminal justice system are primarily responsible for the persons who are in psychiatric crisis.

Without therapy, intervention, or the use of modern medications and treatment modalities, these seriously mentally ill prisoners frequently become difficult to manage. Their disruption is often treated by putting them in eight-by-six-foot disciplinary isolation cells. The extreme deprivation of solitary confinement, and its twenty-three-plus hours-a-day confinement, is enough to push most mentally ill inmates over the edge. In New York State, the average stay for the mentally ill in solitary confinement is three years—and, if this punishment does not pacify an inmate, he can be forced to eat, for up to thirty days, what is known as the "loaf"—a one-pound brick made from bread and potatoes and served with raw cabbage and water—three times a day. This punishment is reminiscent of the observations made by Dorothea Dix. It would appear that we have come full circle.

My concern for mentally ill prisoners is not born from academic concern. While incarcerated in a mental health unit of a federal prison, I was stabbed by another inmate. For my protection, I was locked down in what the state calls a "secure housing unit"—and what the prisoners call "the box," "the hole," or simply "the SHU" (secure housing unit). I spent 40 days in the box while prison guards tried to determine who my assailant was. They failed, and because of my physical and mental deterioration, I was shackled from head to foot and taken to another prison where I was again placed in a SHU, this time for ten days of observation. The secure housing unit is a seemingly endless row of small claustrophobic cells, each with its own steel sink and toilet. Against one wall there is a metal rack covered by a thin, oil-covered pad. This is the bed.

The door is solid steel with a vertical slot that allows a guard to peer in. A small, knee-high horizontal slot is used to deliver and return food trays. The walls are made of concrete cement blocks. Light comes in from a very small barred window and a large fluorescent light that is on all day and part of the night.

When you are in the box, you are confined for twenty-three hours a day, and although you are allowed one hour in the daylight, that hour is spent in an outdoor zoo-like cage where you are often taunted by the other prisoners. I, like most of the inmates in the box, opted to stay inside for the full twenty-four-hour period, hoping to sleep—because sleep at night is next to impossible. That's when the noises begin.

I heard them all night long. One of my neighbors, called "Dogman" by the guards, howled until the dawn like a wounded canine; another kept shouting "Shut up!"; still another sang a tuneless melody with words that spoke of "silver threads and golden needles"; and some engaged in loud conversations with voices that only they could hear. After several weeks of not being able to separate night from day, I too began to hallucinate.

This treatment of the seriously mentally ill is not only horrendous, it also creates a real societal danger. Nationally, there are currently 645,000 mentally ill persons on probation—they have served their time and are back out on the street. Many are more dysfunctional and dangerous than when they were arrested.

Along with many others, I worked hard to have the New York State legislature prohibit the practice of placing the seriously mentally ill in solitary confinement. The legislature was responsive. When the bill was placed on Governor Pataki's desk, I asked for an appointment to see him—to urge him to sign the legislation into law—but Governor Pataki, whom I had sworn into office on two prior occasions, refused to see me. With his eye on national office, and not wanting to be perceived as "soft on criminals," he vetoed the legislation. Fortunately, the New York State legislature again passed the legislation and Governor Spitzer promised to sign the bill into law. This is a much-needed reform; however, it does not address the far more significant problem presented, in which the penal system is, by default, the caretaker of so many of America's mentally ill.

It would be grossly unfair to blame the tragic treatment of the mentally ill prisoner on the corrections system. In New York, the number of state psychiatric beds has dramatically decreased, concurrent with the rise of correctional beds in this state. When I became chief judge in 1985, there were some 35,000 inmates in our state prisons—there are now over 63,000. Between 1983 and 1990, New York State built twenty-seven new prisons at a cost of $5.5 billion, for which the citizens of New York are still paying. At the same time, this state was closing our psychiatric hospitals, going from a commitment high of 93,000 patients in 1955 to its present population of 4,000.

It was with the advent of new psychoactive drugs and improved outpatient modalities that New York and many other states began closing psychiatric hospitals. It was thought that community resources were not available or adequate to absorb this population. The elimination of the psychiatric beds was disastrous for tens of thousands of New Yorkers, many of whom moved into squalid and dangerous single-room-occupancy apartments in poor neighborhoods, homeless shelters, adult homes unprepared to serve them—or the street. Many of the mentally ill in these situations end up in our jails and prisons.

Every effort should be made to see to it that most persons who are seriously mentally ill are not put in prison. Individuals who are seriously mentally ill who have not committed a serious violent crime should be treated and not incarcerated. By the same token, seriously mentally ill murderers, rapists, and others who have committed serious violent crimes, who are competent and not interposing an insanity defense, should be in prison but not deprived of humane and medically appropriate treatment.

New York has established mental health courts in many areas of this state. These courts, with the consent of the accused and the district attorney, are empowered to adjudicate matters involving mentally ill defendants. The goal of these courts is to direct the severely mentally ill defendant to a treatment facility rather than a jail or prison.

The problem with our state's mental health courts is that most defense attorneys will not submit the mentally ill defendant to the jurisdiction of those courts if his client is charged with a misdemeanor—he feels it his obligation to get his client "off" without the need for follow-up treatment, medication, or therapy. On the other hand, if the crime is a felony, it is often the district attorney who will not agree to the matter being brought before a mental health court.

A notable exception to this practice has been charted by Charles J. Hynes, the Brooklyn district attorney. District Attorney Hynes has consented to allowing the submission of felony offenders, even second felony offenders, to the jurisdiction of the mental health court judge to keep hundreds of seriously mentally ill defendants out of prison and direct them to treatment. The success of this program is attested to by the drop in recidivism and the dramatic number of successful case depositions. The mental health courts and the district attorneys dealing with mentally ill defendants would be even more successful if the necessary facilities for crisis intervention and for the housing of those seriously mentally ill defendants, who cannot be housed in the community, were made available.

With the agreement of the New York commissioner of mental health; the deputy secretary for public safety for the State of New York; Judith Kaye, the present chief judge of the State of New York; the chief administrative judge of the State of New York; and the district attorneys of Queens, Nassau, and Kings counties, I have proposed that a pilot program be inaugurated involving those three counties and Creedmoor Psychiatric Center.

Our failure to deal with the current conditions of the mentally ill in our prisons can only be addressed by a renewed and innovative emphasis on diversion and treatment. I feel the suggested pilot program could provide a template that could be replicated on a statewide and even a national basis. Without this use and improvement of existing facilities and systems, we cannot hope to effectively and humanely deal with the existing problem implied in the incarceration of the mentally ill, nor the reasonable expected influx of the mentally ill into our criminal justice system.

It has been fifteen years since my release from prison. I still receive psychiatric care. I still teach—I now have all the speaking engagements I can handle. It has been said that "one door closes and another door opens." That may be true, but it is hell in the hallway. I still feel the pain of rejection from those who do not, and never will, forgive me for my transgression. However, I am most fortunate to have been given the opportunity and privilege of continued public service. Mario Cuomo, a friend whom I admire, asked me what I wanted more than anything. I told him, "Redemption." He said that redemption can only be conferred in heaven. I hope he is wrong.

“Albert Einstein didn’t change the world, he just defined it more accurately.”

THE JOURNEY OF THE WISE

WHAT IS THE DIFFERENCE between knowledge and wisdom? Some people put it this way: Knowledge is knowing that tomatoes are fruit; wisdom is knowing not to put tomatoes in fruit salad. Knowledge will get you on *Jeopardy!*; wisdom will mean your thoughts will be quoted for centuries. Knowledge can get man to the moon; wisdom is making that a useful thing to do. (After all, we have a lot of rocks right here on Earth.) Knowledge can be stacked up like bricks. Wisdom can blow away in a strong wind.

The dictionary is not much help. Wisdom is defined by *Webster's* to mean "the quality of being wise; knowledge, and the capacity to make due use of it; knowledge of the best ends and the best means; discernment and judgment; discretion; sagacity; skill; dexterity." It seems to be intimately linked to knowledge, doesn't it? Yet knowledge is defined as "the state or fact of knowing; familiarity, awareness, or understanding gained through experience or study." What's the difference? Knowledge can be reduced to information, but wisdom can't. Knowledge is available to everyone, yet wisdom is not. Knowledge can be put into any computer, yet the smartest people in the world have demonstrated, time and again, that wisdom is much more elusive. Knowledge is easy; wisdom may be the most difficult thing in the world to attain. Millions of people seek wisdom but settle for information, the cheapest form of knowledge. How to achieve wisdom? The question has been the goal of thinkers and philosophers from the beginning of recorded history.

In the realm of knowledge, information is king. It is widely believed that the acquisition of large amounts of data constitutes knowledge. Yet there are plenty of bartenders who have massive amounts of information at their fingertips and work for tips. There are many scientists, engineers, businessmen, and academics who can claim large amounts of knowledge, yet they can't match their socks, don't notice that their kids are on drugs, and run over the tricycles in their driveways through distraction. Are they not smart, are they not knowledgeable? Of course they are. But their knowledge cannot help them take on the many, many challenges they face every day, including things that are right under their noses. And in a world exploding with information, simple knowledge has lost usefulness. While it has expanded access to knowledge, Google has done little for wisdom in the world.

As *Webster's* says, wisdom is not only knowledge, but the "capacity to make due use of it." What is due use? Due use is knowing what needs to be done, knowing how to do it, and most importantly, knowing why it is important to do. Doesn't everyone struggle with that? How many people wonder not only how to do something but also whether it is the right thing to do? How many wonder, unsure if they are on the right track? How many are gripped by the fear that they have been on the wrong road for a long time, but don't know what to do about it? Their only option, it seems, is to plow forward, repeating the same thing they've been doing for as long as they've been doing it, hoping against hope that they were right…but no longer sure.

It's a horrible way to live—in uncertainty. How can you be sure that you have chosen your course wisely, and that you have the knowledge to carry it out?

First things first. Wisdom is knowing that you can confront your basic assumptions and that this confrontation will not cause your house to fall in. Wisdom is knowing that, whatever mistakes you have made, if you are aware of them, you can cope with them. Wisdom is knowing that, whatever anyone has done to you, as long as you deal with the problem that they have created for you and do not treat them as mortal enemies, you can almost always overcome whatever difficulty they have caused you. Wisdom is knowing that the fear of thinking you were wrong should be acknowledged, and that the solution almost never requires that you do the same thing over again. Wisdom always tends toward accepting new ideas, accepting change, accepting mistakes, and forging something new from them. Knowledge is simply knowing how to go about achieving it.

Many people are convinced of things they "know." Yet one of the most repeated phrases in English, one that seems indispensable to every young person in America, is a cry for understanding, a plea for shared appreciation, a desperate begging for someone else to acknowledge that what they "know" is, in fact, a fact. Who hasn't noticed the increased frequency of the question, "You know?"

What is this if not the uncertainty that so many feel every day? How many adults have to restrain themselves from asking it, understanding the desperation and insecurity that the phrase demonstrates? Yet so many find themselves drawn to it over and over, using it as punctuation.

Yes, many do "know" what is being said at any given time. They can understand the words being said. But how many listen to the deeper things that people say? How many notice the fears and insecurities that we all share? How many are truly aware of the depths of the feelings that others have? Is it any surprise, then, that people keep asking that question?

The multiplication of ways that we now have to communicate with each other has not helped. BlackBerries, Bluetooth, instant messaging of all kinds, and, of course, cell phones have all appeared in the last few years to make it easier and faster to communicate anything to anyone instantly anywhere in the world. Yet humans misunderstand each other as much now as ever. How did this happen?

One reason that it has happened is that we are in a continual race with our technology. We are delighted with it when it first appears, we use it eagerly, we discover new uses for it. But much more thought goes into how to make these external media work *for* us than trying to understand what changes they make *to* us. This is a great demonstration of the difference between wisdom and knowledge. We "know" how to talk to anyone. Do we know what to say? Does the fact that we can communicate so easily make what we have to communicate any more important? Not really. Why? Because we don't know the difference between big "W" and big "K."

To find out the difference between these two concepts and how they affect us, we must start by asking ourselves basic questions. Why am I doing what I'm doing? Why am I working this job? Is this the only job I can get? Can I afford to quit and look for something else? These questions are often so scary that people will go to endless lengths to avoid asking them. Yet until they are faced, and faced squarely, almost no other questions can be answered. Why am I single? Why am I married? Why do I let my significant other walk all over me? What am I lacking that I can't stand up for myself? Ask these questions first. Then, the hard part. Answering them. Here is the path to wisdom.

Face your fears. How many of the great books of wisdom over the centuries have advocated this simple act?

Simple, I say, without having any illusions about how hard this truly is. Facing that which causes you fear takes courage. And courage is not always available. That is why the first step toward wisdom is understanding this very thing: that what you want to change has resisted your attempts to change it in the past. What makes you think this time will be any different? If you don't think about it in new ways, it won't. That's what takes courage. To grapple with your problems in ways that you never have before is to take real emotional and psychological inventory. What can you handle? What can't you handle? What solutions have you groped for in the past? If they failed, what mistake did you make? How did you misunderstand the problem? You must be absolutely ruthless with yourself at this stage. Look at what you thought were the solutions of your past. Did you really understand what you were doing?

Most solutions are found, like most new inventions, not by inventing something new to "handle" a problem. They are found by someone envisioning the problem in a new way. For centuries Newtonian physics worked just fine. Everyone could be made to understand gravity. But for some really inquisitive minds, it was discovered that Newton couldn't answer all questions. This meant reimagining the universe and the laws that held it together. Does anyone believe it was easy to tell people that Newton, the gold standard of geniuses, was wrong? Even a little bit? It took an obscure German physicist working in a Swiss patent office to write the papers that shook the world. Albert Einstein didn't change the world, he just defined it more accurately. The result? Quantum mechanics, atomic energy, and the twentieth century with all its beauty and horror. To call it a scientific revolution is to understate what happened.

Well, everyone can have a revolution in his or her own life. You don't need to shave your head, or move to Tahiti, or take up astrology—all you have to do is look at your problems honestly. Honestly. Including understanding the mistakes you have made. As President Kennedy said, "A mistake only becomes a blunder if you fail to correct it." This means simply that if you can see the problem you have, in all its dimensions, most of the time it is susceptible to correction. Ignoring it, or hoping it goes away, or pretending that it is not really a problem—these are sure ways of perpetuating it. Confront your fears. They are never as big in reality as you make them in your head.

Another step on the path of wisdom is to overcome the problems that certain people cause you. Whether they are people you work with or members of your own family, eventually everyone has a problem with someone else. Is it really a problem with the person? Or is it the person's demeanor, or attitude, or manner, or even smell that bothers you? Is it really necessary to hate someone, someone you know, if you make an honest effort to understand that person? In many cases, "enemies" can be co-opted; they can be made to change their behavior if you are persuasive enough. Angry confrontations that lead nowhere are familiar to all of us. But how many solutions are forged between people who were once enemies? "Politics make strange bedfellows," is an old truism…about politics. Yet if you examine many of the most difficult political decisions in history, you will find that they emanate from a coalition of once-implacable enemies. (The first American senators to go to Vietnam after many years of no relations between our countries? John Kerry and John McCain, two veterans of that war.) In your own life it should be possible to deal with people who have caused you pain without inflicting even more of it. Aren't most disputes amenable to reason? And isn't the first person to propose a way toward peace usually the one who is hailed as the wise one?

Knowledge built intercontinental ballistic missiles, but wisdom kept us from using them. Knowledge took us to the moon during what was called the Space Race, a mortal competition with the Russians that consumed the United States for decades. Wisdom built the International Space Station, with the Russians. Knowledge cracked the genetic code, but wisdom uses it to cure illness.

You may know how to deal with the immediate problems you face every day. But the larger questions are too daunting; they're better left to "experts." People defer to experts, to political and religious leaders, even to celebrities as a way to pass the buck. They don't want to be responsible for, say, global warming. But how many people would be willing to do something about problems we all face if they could be shown a simple, effective means of doing so? Thirty years ago the conversion from leaded to unleaded gasoline was thought to be the end of the automobile industry. "We won't be able to go fast enough!" and "Americans hate catalytic converters! They'll never accept them for just a few miles per gallon!" A lot of money was spent to keep lead in gasoline. Yet here we are, unleaded, in a much cleaner environment than we had thirty years ago. Are you embarrassed that your car won't go faster? Not in America. And all it took was the political will to get it done.

The same thing can be applied to any individual life. Yes, there are long-term, seemingly unsolvable problems we all have. Is anything improved by shrugging? No. Are there problems that truly can't be solved? Again, let's consider history. Three hundred years ago the problem of witches and the presence of Satan was considered so imminently dangerous that many innocent people were put to death in trying to solve the problem. Result? Fear. Solution? Well, there may be fewer witches today, but we are not any better at identifying them than people were in Salem. Two hundred years ago the problem of slavery was thought to be too intractable to eradicate. Result? It took a civil war to change the system, but change it did. Solution? Anyone seen the White House lately? One hundred years ago the problem of aviation had been solved…but the United States was so uninterested that the Wright brothers had to go to Europe to get government financing. Result? Aviation was first used in a massive way to make war. Solution? After two world wars increasingly dominated by aviation, the international civil aviation industry has made travel to the remotest parts of the world commonplace.

History is a good place to see the changes in the world. But public history is only one part of the story. In order to understand all the changes that have taken place, you have to consider not only what the big decisions were, or when the great turning points took place, but the human attitudes behind them. One hundred years may seem like a long time in history, but it was during the time of most peoples' grandparents and great-grandparents. Not so long ago.

Likewise, an individual life is subject to history, too. To really appreciate who you are, you must consider where you have been—emotionally, psychologically, and in every other way. However much you may believe otherwise, you are not the same person you were just a few years ago. Have you noticed the changes? How do you account for them? Have they helped you adapt better? Or hindered you? When you take stock of your life it is important to ask these questions, but even more important is not to settle for the same old answers. You have established patterns throughout your life, the purposes of which were to help you cope. But old patterns, even successful ones, are dangerous. They suggest that you have a way to face a new situation, a tried-and-true method for dealing with a new problem or a confusing situation. But new situations often require new solutions. How do you achieve a truly new solution? By avoiding the patterns of the past. Is this easy? Never. Discarding or replacing something that still seems to work is hard for anyone to do.

Buying a new car (or a different car) is something everyone in America eventually does. Do you want your new car to be better than your old one, or not? Wouldn't you rather have a new car that gets better mileage, that requires less maintenance, that burns less oil, and so forth, or would you rather, for the sake of familiarity, stay with the old one? Or worse, get one that seems new but has all the exact same characteristics as the old one? Real progress can only come through change that is an improvement on the ways things were done before. Real progress can seem scary or uncomfortable at first, but real progress is the only way to adapt to a constantly changing world in a positive way.

Many people hang on to models of the past as a way of proving that they successfully negotiated a particular moment in their lives. This model, or pattern, is something they are proud of—and rightly so. But how often do those old models work on the new problems you face today? How often do we insist on the past, in all its glory, rather than look for real, profound, and meaningful improvement? It takes experimentation, it takes teamwork, it takes innovation, but if history is any judge, progress can be achieved. It cannot be achieved without a price.

Business schools often use the model of the buggy whip industry. One hundred twenty years ago, just before the development of the automobile, buggy whips were understood to be absolutely indispensable. Everyone who aspired to "respectability" had a buggy and the horses to pull it. Factories produced buggy whips in huge quantities, salesmen touted them everywhere, advertising was designed around them, and promotions of all kinds were used to sell them. Buggy whip companies made a lot of money. They were publicly traded, and their stocks were measured just like stocks are measured today. How many of these important companies can you name today?

The resistance to change is often understandable. The future can be scary. In the late 1890s a doctor was rushed to the scene of a horrible new disaster: a car crash. In fact, a pedestrian had been hit by a car and killed. The doctor was horrified. After examining the body, he got up, shaken, and announced that the victim was dead. "I think if everyone knew the horror of what I have just witnessed, they would renounce these infernal machines forever!" he declared. Imagine his shock and dismay as he saw these "infernal machines" not only not be rejected but embraced with every passing day. And in those days the top speed of a car rarely passed twenty miles an hour! What would that good doctor think of us today?

Was he right? Well, he was right to be horrified. It showed a strong conscience and an acute sense of the danger these new inventions posed. But where would we be without cars? Our world is completely shaped by them. The policies of nations and continents are determined by them, and have been for decades now. Could we really return to a time before cars? No more than we can return to any time in our past and resurrect it as a replacement for the present. We can no more renounce cars than we can renounce Einstein or the Emancipation Proclamation. Yet for many people, the fear of the future makes them not only nostalgic for the past but also militant about enforcing it. Any change becomes threatening. All innovation is viewed with suspicion. The good doctor was right, and he was wrong. The solution to the problem was not returning to the era of the buggy whip and horses and stables. The solution was coming up with better safety features in cars, better rules, better training of drivers, better roads, stop lights, stop signs, and traffic enforcement by a well-trained police force. No, these solutions were not easy. They required a lot of work and a complete reorientation of the ways people thought about transportation. But does anyone today doubt that we are better off with the car than relying on horses for us to get around?

It is easy to "know" something. It is much harder being wise. In one's own life it is difficult to change, especially if one has grown comfortable with the way things are. But as they say, a word to the wise: don't expect everything to stay the same, including yourself. The patterns of the past may be comfortable, as rich buggy whip manufacturers must have been, but they rarely prepare you for the challenges of the future. Wisdom is understanding that, no matter how well things have worked in the past, the future will certainly require profound change. Are you ready for it?

“The world’s ‘broken’ includes most of us, but many of us don’t know we can change.”

"LOST AND FOUND"
—PAULA WHITE

TRANSFORMING A LIFE MEANS acknowledging the past, building on its lessons, growing from them, and moving on. Easier said than done, at least for some of us. That's because too often, we go through life without thinking, without learning, and without changing. Then we wonder why we're unable to reach our potential.

Like lemmings, many people instinctively, mindlessly keep going the same direction they've always gone. If lemmings reach a cliff as they migrate, the urge to keep going is so strong that they simply fall off the cliff into the water and swim until exhaustion or death. So it is with some of us. Those who get stuck in their instinctual path easily become the unconscious victims of this conditioned impulse—one that we fail to recognize. I see so much of this in my ministry:

- A sexually abused young girl grows up with internal hostility and wonders why she cannot enjoy sex with her husband.
- The young man with an alcoholic father grows up judging himself without mercy and despairs of ever being content.

- The hyper-critical wife maintains her stance to avoid the powerlessness she felt with her father, but drives her husband and children far from the intimacy her heart desires.

The world's "broken" includes most of us, but many of us don't know we can change. Or, if we do know we can, we don't want to. Change is frightening. It's intimidating. It's hard. So we make excuses, such as "that's just the way I am" or "life is just this way."

Or we pop antidepressants. Or drink. Or drug.

I was once one of those broken people.

My story started one long-ago night, a night that set me traveling down a painful road of my own.

My mother, brother, and I hadn't lived in Memphis long when I heard the knock on the door that terrible night. At first, I was thrilled to hear my father's familiar voice—but it didn't take long for me to recognize that something was different. He sounded harsh and cold. A few words of conversation were exchanged. Then, suddenly, in a panic-stricken tone, my mom screamed, "No! You can't have her!"

The next thing I knew, one of my arms was being yanked and pulled by my daddy and the other arm was being pulled by my mommy. Like a rag doll in a tug-of-war, I was being fought over.

I heard Daddy say, "Let me have her or I'll kill myself!"

"No!" my mother screamed. With every ounce of her strength she held me as if she were holding on to her own life.

Then it was over. The police came and took him away.

I was five years old. In the end, my father took his life just as he had vowed to do. I was devastated.

Until that night, I had lived a somewhat charmed life. My parents were entrepreneurs who owned toy and craft stores—and, as far as I could see from my perspective as a hopeful and naïve child, I was the most fortunate little girl in the world.

My daddy took me to breakfast almost every day. My mother was a hard worker. Lack seemed nonexistent—and whatever problems occurred under the surface of our happy domestic existence, they were invisible to me; my parents shielded me from life's pain.

The harsh reality of my father's death seemed like the ultimate abandonment. It shook me to my core and caused me to question my self-worth. Everyone had always told me that I was the apple of my daddy's eye, but if he loved me so much, why did he leave me? Was it my fault?

Daddy was gone, and I took that as evidence that something had to be wrong with me. I was too young to understand, so I concluded that he left because I was unlovable. I had no way of knowing the impact of this life turn. I couldn't know that I had been set on a path to prove to the world that even though Daddy had left me, I really *was* lovable.

We had been moderately comfortable, but after Daddy's death our economic status changed drastically. My mother now worked long, hard hours. I didn't see her much, and there were always babysitters, often young girls and boys from the neighborhood. My friends were out playing innocent childhood games like hide-and-seek and "red rover." But some of my babysitters had other games in mind. Seeing my vulnerability, they began to take advantage of my need for love and acceptance.

I was only six years old the first time they abused my little girl's body.

In the weeks and years that followed, the abuse happened again and again. These violations—coupled with the abandonment and rejection of my father's death—fostered anguish in my heart so deep that I couldn't help but conclude, again, that it was my fault. This was what I deserved.

All behavior in our lives stems from the beliefs we have about the world around us. In my life, the things that I had counted on crumbled or disappeared. I was a terrified little girl whose world was as dark place, who didn't understand why these things were happening to her.

Seeing the world as a dangerous and hostile place, not surprisingly I became a chronic bed wetter, afraid of the dark, and introverted. As I grew older, I developed perfectionist tendencies, eating disorders, and depression. I entered unhealthy relationships and could measure my self-worth only by my ability to accomplish. I was the classic overachiever: a straight-A student, an award-winning gymnast, and someone who would do whatever it took to gain acceptance and love.

In that quest to find love, I conceived a child out of wedlock.

I kept going down that path, not realizing that things could be different. I was like those lemmings heading for the cliff and swimming mindlessly in a never-ending cycle. Perhaps it would have turned out that way—but at the age of eighteen, I had a defining moment. One afternoon, during a routine visit with a friend, I had an unexpected encounter.

The friend's uncle had come to town and we were sharing some sweet tea, a few good laughs, and conversation. All at once, he turned to me and abruptly asked, "Aren't you tired of your life? Don't you want to know real love?"

I had no idea where these questions were coming from. *Of course*, I thought to myself, taken aback, *but how could he have known?*

Although his questions had come from left field and seemed inappropriate in such a casual setting, I had an inexplicable sense that this man knew something—that he was going to reveal something to me that would alter my life forever. Casual conversation or not, I felt there was something special in that moment. It was an unforgettable moment and I remember it vividly to this day.

By then I had become a master at disguising my feelings and covering up any trace of pain or problems—or so I thought. But as my heart began to pound, I felt a question rise from deep within: *Would I keep on pretending everything was okay forever, while inside I was lost and desperately hurting?* I knew there was something real and alive inside of me, something good, but I had no idea how to find it.

Still, I wanted my life and my world, as I had come to know them, to change—for the better. Perhaps this was my chance.

The uncle looked me in the eye. "Well," he said, "I have the answer to your problems and the solution to your pain."

I was still wondering how he'd even known I was searching, when he opened up a book that I later learned was a Bible.

I had never been to church before. The name Jesus, to me, was no different from Tooth Fairy or Santa Claus. I'd heard the name but didn't know anything about him. I was more than a little curious. How was Jesus the solution to my pain?

I will never forget the moment that man began to share with me words of life—truths that penetrated through the labels, life experiences, and limitations placed on me by the world, and more importantly, the ones I had placed on myself.

As my friend's uncle took me on a journey through the Scriptures, my eyes were opened, and for the first time in my life, I began to know and understand the power of true love. Soon after that day, I remember holding up a Bible and saying, "God, I don't know you. I don't even know myself. But I want to."

And from that afternoon evolved my two-year exploration of the Word, and my ongoing, ever-evolving transformational journey with Christ.

I began to understand for the first time that we are all unique and special in God's eyes. He has a specific destiny and purpose for each of us. I began to learn that I could be everything that He created me to be, that I didn't have to let my past dictate my future. As I continued to study the word of God,

I learned that my self-labels were wrong and unnecessary. I began to understand the meaning of Christ's unconditional love. I recognized that, more than anything, I wanted to spend the rest of my life helping people know and realize the same love and joy He had brought into my life.

My outreach ministry actually began one Thanksgiving. Someone gave me a turkey and I cut it in half. I saved one part for my son, Brad, and me. I made turkey sandwiches and brought them to the homeless with the other half. The feeling I got from that gift was indescribable. On that day I knew beyond a shadow of a doubt that I was called to help and minister to people. That modest offering was the beginning of my own transformation.

From there, I began doing volunteer work in the inner city and realized that every time I stooped over to hug a little girl or offered food to a homeless person, a little piece of me healed. God was transforming me.

I kept it up—every day doing what God put before me. From there God blessed me with a church, a global television ministry that potentially reaches 2.3 billion people every day, and unfathomable opportunities to minister to influential leaders and history makers worldwide. It wasn't a direct path, or a short one. But it was a clear one, and one I continue to walk down every day as God provides direction. He has greater plans for each of us than we can imagine. He may not call you to minister, but He has a unique plan and purpose for your life.

People often ask me, "Paula, how can I discover God's plan for me?"

Here's my answer: Learn to listen to that small, still voice inside you. Learn to recognize the opportunities God puts in front of you. Understand that you do not have to be limited by old self-definitions, by the story of your past. You can create a new future. Don't be afraid to step out and move on. Examine your limits. Test your limits. And most of all, appreciate God's many gifts in your life.

Everyone has problems. It's just a matter of degree. You may not have been abused, your daddy may not have died, but you too have your own story. No one's life is perfect. Obstacles in your path do not mean it is over. You can almost always find a way around an obstacle. The secret is to not give up. Reach out, ask for help, pray. Take the time you need to think it through, work it through.

I have learned firsthand that God gives us all the opportunity to become fruitful and to live according to His unique plan for our lives. It is our responsibility to discover that plan. That takes a conscious awareness of ourselves, our gifts, and a willingness to deal with the limitations that we put upon ourselves. It's easy to sit back and have a pity party. The hard work is to actually live consciously and fully. This is the difference between living completely or just following. Consciousness will lead to a plan. And when you find that unique plan God has for you, pursue it with passion.

And by the way, that child I conceived when I was eighteen? Today he is a college graduate and the greatest gift God has ever given me. I've always counseled him to find his passion in life and to pursue it with everything he has in him.

Remember, no matter what your circumstances, you are always precisely positioned for God to act in your life, to shed His light on your situation, for Him to help you discover your path. Life is filled with challenges and opportunities, and I believe that each of us can be equipped to victoriously face them all. I truly believe that what may seem like our worst stumbling blocks can be the stepping stones to our greatest successes.

“The most difficult thing to explain is that which is obvious.”

PERSEVERANCE: THE SELF-CORRECTION PRINCIPLE

HOW DOES ANYONE SURVIVE the traumas and dramas, the triumphs and failures of life? Anyone who has lived has had to survive the terrible, seemingly inevitable difficulties that life throws at us. Accidents and abuse, neglect and discrimination, mistakes and missed opportunities—these drown our ordinary lives like so much flooding after a monsoon. And no matter how well prepared you are, no matter how strictly you adhere to surefire standards of conduct, no matter how hard you try to peer around corners, something always happens to upset and overturn the most carefully laid plans.

People respond to these problems in a bewildering variety of ways. Some are crushed. They were sure they had foreseen every possibility—except the one they now face. This realization is too much for them. They cannot recover from the loss they experience, or the accident that derails them, or the unexpected change of circumstances that, in fact, were *not* foreseen. Faced with a reality they have not prepared for, they find themselves adrift in a world they no longer understand. They respond badly, lashing out at "others," blaming murky adversaries ("*they* are responsible!"), and generally behaving like victims. They grow righteous and more extreme, and they seek to externalize what they cannot internalize—their own mistakes. Hence, we have "they" to blame.

Other people respond differently. They realize that their plans, however well-laid, are never perfect. They understand that part of the process of any venture, including the venture of life, will include unexpected surprises. They appreciate that they may have made a mistake—in judgment, in understanding, or in trust—that they must correct if the situation is to improve. And that is the key, the biggest difference between those who blame others and those who seek their own solution: the ability to self-correct.

What does it take to do this? What do you do when faced with a problem that has already defeated you once? How do you recover? The short answer is perseverance; that is, getting back up after you've been knocked down. The secret that every successful person will tell you is not so secret after all. Simply put, it is this: experience tells you that you have already overcome many, many problems to get to this point, so experience should tell you to be confident in your own abilities to overcome this one.

That's it. Experience. Experience should show you that you were not always right in the past. Granted, you may be facing a problem exponentially bigger than any you have faced in the past. But you are the one who survived to this point, so why give up now? Giving up guarantees only one outcome—the state you are in. Is that good enough? Is defeat more comfortable than whatever you might face by trying again? Many people think so, which is how the media profits so enormously by catering to the permanently embittered. But for many others, defeat is not a comfortable option. We are bound to try again, sometimes by circumstances and not by choice. But since we are bound to try again, shouldn't we organize our thinking accordingly? Can you persevere while nursing a grudge? No. Can you teach yourself to persevere? Yes.

Perseverance means to try again. Moreover, it means to try again despite obstacles. Some people prefer the obstacles to the solutions. They fall in love with obstacles, in fact. Obstacles are so much easier to rail against and denounce, and they are an excuse to give in to the most damaging of all emotions—hate. But perseverance exists despite obstacles. It means not being detoured from your purpose. It means taking control of your future instead of leaving it in the hands of fate. Perseverance means taking realistic stock of your situation, however different it is from the one you anticipated, and making adjustments. In some cases, this means accepting a smaller role for yourself than you may have wanted. In others, it means reframing the problem in a way that changes its meaning. In some cases it is making lemonade from lemons, and in others it is figuring out that oranges taste better and are just as good for you. Hanging on to old solutions is not an option, because the old solutions led you to the situation you're in. New solutions, some of which you might have discarded out of hand, are necessary.

The solution to being a buggy whip manufacturer in a world of cars is not to make a better buggy whip. The solution is to figure out what these darned auto-mobiles are all about, anyway, and to work with that. It didn't take long for the market to teach this lesson to buggy whip makers. But how many of them had already made the leap themselves? How many actually absorbed the lesson before they went bankrupt? How many just railed about those "infernal machines"? Yes, maybe it was too late to become Henry Ford by then, but wasn't there room for other good ideas? Weren't new entrepreneurs rewarded for those good ideas in the world of cars? This would be useful advice today, considering the ongoing trauma of the U.S. automobile industry. The point is not that automobiles are the perfect example of innovation and imagination, but that people came up with the ideas, persevered, and made it possible to increase our size, speed up our transportation, and change our world.

One problem with perseverance is the problem of perception. If someone has failed once, it would only seem logical for others to assume that they are failures. But to perceive someone as a failure for making one mistake is to paint with too broad a brush. It precludes any possibility of that person returning, overcoming, and making a new, successful life. It sticks that person with a permanent label in an impermanent world. If we know that change is inevitable, then doesn't it follow that failure is inevitable, at least for some? It should also follow, then, that most people have failed at something at one time or another. Are they all failures? Forever?

Perceptions lead to labels. Can people be labeled? Pollsters and marketers certainly hope so. But the truth is that, however apt a label might be, people are rarely one thing all the time. People react to things in the most diverse ways. They depend on their perceptions of things to guide their decisions. But perceptions are tricky. They are not always true. Doctors don't want to hurt their patients, but they sometimes prescribe the wrong drugs or the wrong dosages because they have the wrong information. Politicians rarely want to hurt their constituencies by advocating policies they know to be wrong, but still, sometimes their false assumptions do just that. Mothers don't want to hurt their children by feeding them the wrong food, but somehow we have become the most obese country in the world, beginning with our children. With these kinds of choices, it is easy to become paralyzed with the fear of making the wrong decision. But isn't not making a decision a decision in itself? And isn't the fear of making a wrong decision just as decisive an influence as a wrong decision made with the certainty that it is right? Like I said, it's tricky.

You should not count on a decision made in the past to be right again. It should be forgotten. Just feel secure in the knowledge that you had, indeed, made the right decision. To take a decision for granted is to be stuck with it, whether you are aware of it or not. Once you stop examining your beliefs, your perceptions, and your solutions, you no longer have the ability to change them. By not changing them, you guarantee that they will become outmoded and, worse, counterproductive. All cries to regulate Wall Street before 1929 were greeted with choruses of "Socialism!" Yet when the crash was followed with the Great Depression, many of the same voices supported the creation of the Securities and Exchange Commission.

History is filled with similar flip-flops. To label anything is to put it in an unexamined box and expect it to remain there, unchanged. Is that realistic? No. Yet over and over again it has been shown that ideas, policies, and perceptions rely on unexamined assumptions about the past. These assumptions have often led to the worst crises, yet once they are examined they are revealed to be obvious. In 1979 Americans who were still paying attention were shocked to find that Vietnam and China went to war with each other. This meant that the war that the United States fought to prevent a "Communist Vietnam" under the absolute control of "Communist China" was based on a false assumption. We fought a war to prevent the spread of what we perceived to be an evil ideology. Yet once we were gone (along with our assumptions), it appeared that the ideology was not nearly as decisive as good old-fashioned nationalism. So much for assumptions.

Realistic perceptions would seem to play an important role in making realistic assessments. But how can we count on our own perceptions to be realistic? Worse, if our perceptions have been wrong in the past, how can we be sure we will be right in the future? Again, experience should teach us something. Past failures should be just as illuminating as past successes. What did we get right? What can be salvaged from a disaster? The very least we can do is try to assess our mistakes, assumptions, and perceptions. If life has just knocked you down, it stands to reason that the punch it delivered can be parried next time. The first question any fighter asks after being knocked down is, What hit me? If he can get up, he should ask this question for practical and not rhetorical reasons. What hit me? Once a fighter has the answer to that question, it presupposes that the same punch won't work on him again. He'll be looking for it.

Forewarned is forearmed, they say. This principle works in life as it does in boxing. Forewarned is forearmed, but many people refuse to accept that they were knocked out. They forget how it happened. This happens to boxers, too, but they have the excuse that absorbing a knockout punch actually destroys neurons. What's the excuse for people who have never been in a boxing ring? They prefer to ignore the past, when they "failed." This is not perseverance—this is willfully ignoring the only thing that can help you overcome the defeat you suffered. Because failing to learn from mistakes is a one-way ticket to more defeat. Failing to appreciate how your own perceptions led you to make the mistakes you made is wishful thinking. And it guarantees more of the same. Are you willing to suffer this defeat again, knowing what it cost you in the past? Wouldn't you do anything to avoid repeating that fate? I know I would.

So what does it take to persevere? How do you get back up after being knocked down, often more than once? Sometimes it means plowing ahead. Maybe you were right and the rest of the world hasn't caught up to you. This is not wishful thinking unless you are refusing to accept other people as you have accepted yourself. If everyone around you is stuck on Newton and you have discovered Einstein, should you tailor your assumptions and perceptions just to accommodate others? No. Sometimes you have to persist in your beliefs. If you are sure that you are right, or that your product is right, or that your way of thinking is right, then you have an obligation to pursue it to its conclusion. But if you are not sure, then you have an obligation to trim your sails, adjust your perceptions, and realize that maybe, just maybe, you don't have all the answers.

If you have come to this conclusion already (and let's face it, very few of us can understand Einstein's general idea, much less his math), then what you must do next follows naturally. If you conclude that you were, in fact, wrong about something, which led you to make the wrong decision and caused you to act unwisely, which in turn led to disaster, only then should you start examining your thought processes and perceptions to find the roots of your errors (there is rarely a single one). Once you do this, it is just a matter of time before you can shake off the past and start trying to make a new future.

Perseverance, then, is not some mindless motion forward that refuses to take the past into account. Perseverance is bound to the past, however much it is focused on the future. Perseverance requires that you not go charging blindly toward the same wall you confronted before. At least, not if you expect different results. One collision with reality should be a lesson. Two gives you a concussion and is counterproductive. Almost everything is easier without a headache. Perseverance is coming back from adversity, all right, but not doing so blindly. To overcome adversity means to avoid the pitfalls you have already suffered. New pitfalls may appear, but you won't be going too fast this time. Keep your eyes open just at the moment when you had them closed in the past. Otherwise, guess what? Exactly—the same old headache, or worse.

History repeats itself, they say. This is usually not followed by what concludes the statement, but it should be. This is that history repeats itself, the first time as tragedy, the second time as farce. This is usually coupled with the saying that those who fail to learn their history are doomed to repeat it. Well, this is true not only of history, with its eras and movements and big ideas. It is also true of all of us as individuals. We all have histories. We all remember things about the past. But do we remember them correctly? That is, do we remember them in ways not guaranteed to merely reinforce our old assumptions? Or do we look at the past in ways that challenge our ideas, especially the ones that turned out to be mistakes? If we examine our histories honestly, then we should be able to sort out the good ideas from the bad ones. We should be able to say: I was wrong about that. I won't be wrong about that in the future.

But many people resist this idea of having been wrong once like they resist going to the dentist. It's a dull ache, at first. More and more work must be taken on to distract you from the pain of it. Eventually, even a frenzy of activity cannot erase the terrible feeling you have that something, somewhere, is terribly, terribly wrong. If you are willing to say that you have a toothache, then it should follow that the simple solution is making an appointment with a dentist. It takes courage sometimes to identify the simple reality and act on it. But once it is acted on, once the problem is solved, it is hard not to notice that it wasn't such a big problem after all. It's not easy to bite the bullet (an actual dental solution, once upon a time), but once you do, you can proceed knowing that whatever else happens, at least you don't have the same old problem.

A very wise man once said that the most difficult thing to explain is that which is obvious. How many obvious truths do we avoid every day? Of course, it's possible to go through an entire life without understanding the subtleties of quantum mechanics, derivative markets, or fractal geometry. For many of us, not understanding these things not only does not hinder us from pursuing our lives, but actually makes it easier by removing some of the confusing complexity from that pursuit. But there are obvious truths we avoid every day that are worth reviewing. Will this action actually help me? Is this person actually worth spending the time and effort required for a mutual understanding? How do I make my life happier (not necessarily wealthier)? Have I said "I love you" today? Why not? What action did I take to make the people around me happy? What did I do for myself today? If you are not asking these questions, maybe now is a good time to start.

Perseverance is the key to recovering from any setback. It is the guide and the impulse; it is the knowledge that any obstacle can be overcome, that all problems have solutions, and that you are uniquely empowered to take advantage of your life in all its complexity and difficulty. You are. No one else is. If you appreciate all that life has given to you, both good and bad, then you can persevere with the knowledge that the past is your teacher, not your jailer. To persevere in the face of the terrible obstacles of life is to find new solutions to old problems, to overcome the mistaken assumptions of the past with new assumptions that describe reality more accurately. It is to embrace change because you are confident that your experience, your knowledge, and your flexibility will yield a good outcome from the temporary uncertainty that change brings. If you have persevered in the past and overcome, then you know that your assumptions were not wrong and that pursuing them further will eventually yield the same results. But if you are persevering in something that has caused you problems, even disasters, and you are doing it in the same way, then you are not preparing to overcome obstacles. You are guaranteeing that those same obstacles will stop you again. That is not perseverance, but obstinacy.

Enlightened perseverance is something we all aspire to. Often it is the process that is more important than any outcome. If you appreciate the process of life, you will appreciate that no single approach can provide a final solution to anything. Only by maintaining your flexibility in the face of a changing, impermanent world can you hope to keep your balance. This is not an easy thing to do and shouldn't be mistaken as such. Sometimes it's worth your life's effort to change course. But failing to do so is failing to acknowledge the past. How many of us can really afford to ignore that reality? How many of us actually prefer headaches? Do you?

"I have reconstituted myself, recommitted myself, and pulled myself back together many times. But I have never reinvented myself."

"ORIGINAL BY DESIGN"
—José Eber

FOR MORE THAN THIRTY years I have been well known, even famous, in a business notorious for how quickly it forgets its leading practitioners. I have created styles renowned throughout the world, changed the look of millions of people, published best-selling books, and appeared in all the media. I have made and lost fortunes, I have been applauded by the rich and famous, and I have been misled by the unscrupulous to the point that I have been forced not only to defend my name but sue to reacquire it. I have reconstituted myself, recommitted myself, and pulled myself back together many times. But I have never reinvented myself.

Throughout my eventful life I can say honestly that I have never changed. Despite the upheavals of business and fashion, the competition in a very cutthroat field, and the sharp attention of the not-always-sympathetic press, I have continued to follow my own path, my own character, and my own ideas without variation. In a world that constantly demands change and that is eternally fascinated with the new, I have survived and thrived because I understood who I always was and had been. And I never forgot where I came from.

When I arrived in Los Angeles in 1975 with little more than scissors and a dream, I felt instantly and completely at home. Perhaps it was the similarity with Nice, where I was born and raised—the Mediterranean climate, the proximity of the beach, the palm trees, the glamour so reminiscent of the south of France—whatever it was, I had never felt so quickly and totally integrated in a place. More than these physical elements, though, there was something else that made me feel more comfortable here than in my native Europe. I sensed the spirit of the United States was different, that this was a place where people banked on new ideas and on new personalities. I realized that here I would not have to conform. Here, I would be able to promote a new style, free from the criticism and condescension that was common in Europe.

I grew up in Nice and from the time I was fourteen years old, I knew what I wanted to do. I was always playing with girls' hair, beginning with my sister's and my mother's. I understood that I had a gift, but I also knew that it was hard work. And I already knew, at fourteen, the value of money. My father struggled to support us, and from the time I got my first apprenticeship that same year, the money I brought home was important. My father's struggles made him somewhat aloof and withdrawn. The economic pressure on my family was the permanent undertone to everything in our lives. We were all aware of the precariousness of our situation at every moment. The lesson this taught is with me today: you can never let up, you can never surrender to fear, you can never stop trying to succeed—giving up was not and is not an option.

Along with this lesson I learned something equally important about myself. I learned that conforming was ultimately impossible for me. First my father and then my boss at the first salon where I worked in Paris insisted that I cut my hair. This was in the 1960s, and long hair was becoming an important way for young people to differentiate themselves from the previous generation. Looking back over my early years, I see the seeds of transformation and realize that if I had succumbed to the pressure and not expressed my own style, my life would never have turned out the way it did. At the time, I didn't have a plan or a clue about what would come, but I was driven to be an individual. Like so many young people at that time, I was not conscious of creating a new style so much as I was just trying to express my dissatisfaction with what the world expected of me. I grew determined to take control over my own expression, to command my own image. It was as much about growing up and asserting myself as an individual as it was about rebellion.

I chafed at my father's and my boss's strictness. I felt stifled. And the first chance I got, I let my hair grow long. I did not think of it as a "trademark" or a "brand"; for me it was an honest expression of who I felt I really was. It was this feeling, the desire for independence, that drove me as much as any ambitions I might have had. I had determined, from the first time I got the opportunity, never again to allow anyone to tell me who I was or what I should look like. Eventually, I realized that I had discovered something that others coveted—freedom. By insisting on managing my own "look" and letting others know that there was nothing wrong with their "look," I learned that I was not alone, that others also felt stifled by their environments, by their societies, and by the expectations that surrounded them every day. I began to realize that what I had to offer was more than hairstyles, more than a temporary improvement in a person's looks, but a path to self-expression.

Balzac once said, "Behind every great fortune is a great crime." I was sure that was not so. I believed that it was possible to make a great fortune while offering true value to people, without taking advantage of their insecurities or their fears. I believed that if I was honest and worked hard that I would be rewarded. This turned out to be somewhat ingenuous, since business partners were able to take advantage of my goodwill. It cost me a lot of money to realize that others were not as generous as I was. It also became apparent over the years that because I did not want to believe in Balzac's saying—that I was vulnerable to selfishness—I had always felt responsible for and to others. My family, my friends, my employers, and my employees all had claims on my attention, responsibility, and support. I was never able to master the trick of total selfishness, concentrating solely on my own benefit at the expense of everyone else. To live in that way, totally disconnected form everyone else, is a terrible price to pay for wealth. I have always been sure that, whatever happens to me, I will not give in to this pressure. As I said, it has cost me a lot of money to retain my principles. I am happy to say that I am not disappointed in the result.

Within a short time of my arrival in Los Angeles I established myself as an innovative creator of hairstyles. I was invited by one of the city's leading hairstylists to join his salon. Soon I was the driving force behind the Maurice José salon. I began getting referrals from the leading ladies of Hollywood. Susie Coelho, who was married to Sonny Bono at the time, introduced me to many of her girlfriends—Cher, Raquel Welch, Farrah Fawcett, and others. Their hairstyles began to attract attention, and that attention brought the world to me.

I feel now that this success was not an accident. I had a strong work ethic, a high sense of professionalism, and a good eye for style, true. But I also had a conviction about what I was doing. It was my job, as I saw it, to bring out the beauty that existed in everyone. Moreover, I felt that what I did was as important to me as it was to my clients. Years later, an older lady in New York put it best when she told someone, "José didn't make me beautiful—he showed me that I already am." I could never receive a higher compliment, or a more insightful one. To show someone her own beauty has always been my goal, my pride, and my profession. Anyone can cut hair. Beauty must be unearthed, molded, and demonstrated. It must convince one of one's own innate value, and of one's vision of oneself. To show a woman her own beauty in a way that surprises her, yet feels familiar to her, is as much an act of creation as any artist could achieve. And no artist could feel more satisfaction at this than I have.

Perhaps this attitude has caused some of my reversals. I have focused on others, sometimes to my own detriment, but I have never regretted it. The human relationships that I have are well worth the disappointments that I have suffered. After years of effort and constant work, of defining and cultivating and refining my vision, I have finally accomplished what I have often been told was impossible. I am independent in business and as my own person. I am busy preparing for the future. What has caused me to continue? Why do I still work so hard? What is it that compels me to seek new avenues of expression?

I believe that my drive to continue, my endless search for that elusive success, is to prove to myself that my individuality is something valuable. I have, in fact, proved this to myself and to many others, many times over. Yet despite considerable success, the urge to triumph has not diminished. I have never been interested in the opinions others have of me. I have been focused only on expressing in others what I myself have always understood—that everyone is entitled to their own beauty. This "entitlement" (a dirty word these days) is something I hold as precious. That everyone should feel beautiful is something that I believe is sacred. And if this is a value I hold so dear for others, why should I not covet it for myself? To act otherwise—to stop and say, "That's enough, I've done all that I can"—would be a betrayal of my beliefs. There are always more people who have not understood their own value yet. In fact, the numbers seem to increase year by year. To believe that I should rest on my laurels would be an admission of complacency that I do not feel. I am in the middle of my struggle, not at the end.

When a person has found out who he or she truly is, then it is just a matter of time until that person succeeds. It is so important to focus one's energies and abilities in a difficult world, but people often forget what the goal of all the effort is. I have always understood that the goal is to be happy, and that happiness is best achieved through self-expression, and that true self-expression can only be achieved when one has a clear understanding of who one is and what one's place in the world is. I have been lucky, I know, in achieving the success I have achieved. But it was not just luck or talent or drive that allowed me to be successful—it was also understanding myself. This brought the conviction that I was doing something valuable and important, and if I was able to communicate that conviction to others, then today I consider myself as having done the best I possibly could have. In mining the beauty of others, I have been able to convince them not of the power of a hairstyle, but of the power they have over their beauty, and the strength they get from recognizing that beauty.

People search for beauty endlessly, but they often miss their own. Some grow so dismissive of it that they stop looking in mirrors. They grow indifferent to themselves. This must be guarded against at all times. To stop cultivating your beauty is to surrender to the superficial impression others will have of you. If you are aware of your potential for beauty, then you can manage it and nurture it into a powerful source of self-esteem. Once this is done successfully, then it becomes not a privilege but a right. This is something no one should be able to take away from anyone else. No social restrictions should be placed on people who are trying to express themselves and their own beauty. To do so is to rob them of themselves, to prevent them from achieving what everyone should be free to achieve—their own independence. People seek to express themselves in many, many ways. Who can say who is right and who is wrong? At least in the matter of beauty, it doesn't make any sense to limit people's expressiveness. It is an attempt to censor the human spirit, and this is something all people should fight. Be free! Be who you are! And never let anyone tell you who you are. Only you can determine that; only you should define yourself. And only you can ultimately judge yourself.

“Nothing worth achieving was ever achieved by a single person isolated from the rest of humanity.”

HOW TO MAKE HOPE POSSIBLE

FROM THE EARLIEST TIMES of recorded history to the front pages of today's newspapers, it is possible to see a purely human conflict, one that rages in the hearts of people everywhere. This conflict has driven so much of human destiny that it can seem like the one problem that will be with us until the sun finally sputters out. How can a person resolve the ancient tug-of-war between belief, which is the certainty that what you are doing is the right thing to do, and fear, the horrible hollow feeling that robs you of certainty, that drains your courage, and that can paralyze the bravest? To believe in yourself is a gift that only you can give yourself, sometimes in the face of enormous odds. Fear is manufactured in every part of the external world: fears of things seen and unseen, fears about reality, fear of failure, and ultimately, to paraphrase Franklin Roosevelt's immortal words, the fear of fear itself.

Belief and fear wage war in our hearts every day. No one can doubt that they are both necessary, one as an ambitious drive for the future, the other as a warning about the things that have gone wrong in the past. But must they drive us unconsciously? Have we no way to control these two forces?

Are we cursed to live in blind hope or crushing despair, with little middle ground? Or is there a balance? Is there a way to keep belief from running away with us, opening us up to the dangerous blind spots that hope wishes away? Is there a way to keep our fears from overwhelming us with terror, leaving us helpless to confront the realities that we cannot deny or ignore any longer?

Once you begin looking at this problem, it is hard not to see it everywhere. People who believe in certain ideals, whether the free market, democracy, love, or the family, can have their faith tested by things that are out of their control. Economic disasters (politely called "downturns" in the business press) can shake a person's faith in his or her abilities like nothing else. Tell someone who has lost his home that he is part of an economic "correction" and that this is good for the overall picture of real estate prices in the long-term…and you will likely get a punch in the nose. Tell someone who has been laid off that the labor "market" will eventually make a comeback, but in the meantime…and again, you'd better have your self-defense skills up-to-date. When people lose faith in their ability to put food on the table and a keep a roof over their heads, very few external things can repair that damage.

How do you resurrect hope? How can you fight back against the fear that threatens you and yours? Where do you find the strength to get back up after being knocked down? There is a simple answer, but it's hard: you find it in reality.

Fear is an emotion, as hope is, and it has a specific function. Fear is supposed to work as a caution. It's a learned response to bad experiences. Fear is designed so that you have access to memories of the past, memories of how things turned out badly. It is supposed to warn you that what you are embarking on has the potential to be disastrous. Fear uses the store of the past that everyone carries; it activates one's defenses. We need fear. Without fear we would stumble into catastrophe every day. The problem of fear isn't that it exists—

it is an absolutely essential part of our psychological and emotional makeup that we couldn't survive without. The problem of fear is that it can get out of control. It is easy to see catastrophe around every corner. It is easy to feel that everything you try is sure to meet with disaster. In short, it is easy to feel fear about everything. And there is no shortage of reasons for this fear, no shortage of news about the terrible things that happen to people, no shortage of anecdotes available on every corner about how bad things lurk in the shadows for good people. What happens if you give in to this terrible drumbeat that you can hear in the background? What happens if you capitulate to the shadows we all perceive? Well, one thing that will happen is clear—it will never go away.

Fear has a way of sustaining itself and reproducing itself that is viral. It's a simple, primitive emotion that needs little to keep itself alive, exactly like a virus. It can feed on the slightest of diets: asteroids and aliens crashing on Earth, black helicopters mysteriously buzzing over strange places, unexplained disappearances in particular spots in the ocean, rumors of alligators in the sewers, and vanishing frogs. Whether these are explainable or not, they all feed into that primitive, gnawing need we have to worry and fret and brace ourselves when we try to see around invisible corners. Man is the creature most outfitted with foresight and imagination—and these two qualities sometimes reinforce each other in the worst way to produce fear. We all know people who see catastrophe around every one of those corners. *Saturday Night Live*'s Debbie Downer was a comic version of the personality type, but it is common enough for all of us to recognize. On perfectly sunny, beautiful days, some people become convinced that the actual perfection of the day is a trick, that an unexpected monkey wrench is about to be thrown into the works, that this is the moment when a rain of frogs will drown you, or a penny dropped from a skyscraper will land right on you, or a manhole cover will blow you to kingdom come just as you're walking over it.

In its extremes, fear leads to out-and-out paranoia—the conviction that the whole world is organized exactly and down to the last detail with one purpose only: to destroy you. To some extent we are all subject to fear. Very few truly, completely fearless people survive long into adulthood. But if we are all subject to fear, how is it that more of us don't dissolve into quivering, paralyzed zombies whenever we read a headline about a fresh disaster? What pulls us back from the edge and allows us to go to the store for milk despite knowing that Wall Street just crashed (again), gas prices are soaring, the world is warming, wars are raging—and that's just the front page? How do we do it? We do it with fear's antidote and counterbalance: hope.

What is hope? Hope is the belief that, despite all the evidence against trying *anything* in a world as precarious as this one, it is still possible to accomplish *something*. Going to the store for milk might not solve the stock market crash, but in its humble simplicity it does have something important to say about the human spirit. Going to get milk may be homely, but like a lot of homely acts it gets the job done. We need it. We can get it. It is good for us. What did we do? We answered a simple human need. We took stock of the situation, realized we needed something, and somehow, despite the terror and the uncertainty, despite the wars and the aliens, we put our minds to this simple task—and we got it done. How did that happen? With all the reasons in the world to be paralyzed, lying in the fetal position in the darkest corner we can find, somehow we make it out to achieve our basic needs. Is this enough? No. Man cannot live on milk alone. But if we look at it carefully, we can see that it offers us a solution to the problem of fear. Belief that we can do something is just as critical as the certainty that whatever we do is doomed to failure. Before we try to do something—anything—we must believe that it is possible. Despite all the evidence that nothing can be done against the world, which seems organized to thwart us at every opportunity, somehow people have managed to overcome an impressive list of obstacles to get us where we are. This has given us an impressive list of achievements, too. A partial list? Doubling the world's population in 100 years despite war, disease, revolution, and famine. Uninterrupted Olympic games for the last sixty years despite international tensions that threatened the existence of the world. Apollo 11. How were any of those things possible without belief? And belief does not have to take place on a grand scale for its effects to be felt. Belief is necessary in order to have children. It is necessary for starting a business. You can't undertake any significant project without it. So where does it come from? It comes from the same primitive place that fear comes from. And like fear, it is available to everyone. It is as much a part of our human heritage as any emotion, as intimately a part of us as joy or sadness or pleasure or pain. Why, then, does belief in ourselves seem to be harder to come by than fear?

For one thing, it is easier to scoff at "dreamers." People who talk about possibilities always seem to meet a wall of other people prepared to sneer at their "naïvete." These "realists" see the world as it really is, the narrative goes. They are not "taken in" by the "starry-eyed" belief that people trying to forge a different future are "visionaries." No. They are fools, in this formulation. By contrast, realists have their "feet on the ground." They understand that which "dreamers" refuse to acknowledge: that man is a savage dressed up. They "know" that, given the chance, any person would cut another's throat for advantage. Their reflexive cynicism and sour certainty is designed to do what any ideology is designed to do—explain the world. Enough people suffer enough disaster for this mindset to gain some currency, but does it really explain everything? Are all humans motivated solely by their own self-interest? And is that self-interest necessarily and permanently at the expense of another?

Man is a social animal. Humans need other humans. There is enough evidence available to suggest that, by himself and without any assistance, man is a goner. What was ever achieved in perfect solitude? The greatest scientific advancements had to be acknowledged by others before they could achieve their true significance. The most wonderful art is pointless if it goes unperceived by other people. Composers and inventors may work alone, but in order to succeed they must have access to other people. Doesn't it make sense, then, that in order to overcome the most solitary emotion—fear—people should look to other people for solutions?

Belief in yourself alone is never enough. You must believe that you can convince others of your vision to enlist their help. Sometimes this is obvious. The airplane was not invented by Orville or Wilbur Wright, but by the Wright *brothers*. America was not explored by Lewis or Clark, but by Lewis *and* Clark. The structure of DNA was not discovered by Crick or Watson, but by Crick *and* Watson. How did they do it? They believed in themselves and in each other. No revolution can be started, maintained, and brought to its conclusion by a single man. Nothing worth achieving was ever achieved by a single person isolated from the rest of humanity. Of course, by the same token, some of the worst things that man has ever done have been collaborations. But these disasters were overturned in time by the concerted efforts of other groups that rose to combat them. The history of humanity suggests that we are a group of individuals who, whatever our individual fates, work together to achieve what we want to achieve. This means that we depend on one another. It also means that we cannot stop innovating. Each generation must come up with a solution to the fresh problems of the day. Every addition to the human network adds complexity to an already complex world. There are twice as many people today as there were in the time of our great-grandparents, and at that time people were so overwhelmed with the complexity of the era that they could think of no better solution than to try to kill each other at unprecedented rates (see World Wars I and II). Since then, we have developed weapons that would make the happy warriors of that time pale with fear…yet we haven't used them. Isn't that a triumph of collective belief? That we understand now, finally and forever, that we are all connected by this terrible bargain we have with nuclear weapons? The lesson of these terrible weapons is simple: we cannot afford to give in to our worst fears (they will hit us first!) or our most optimistic beliefs (no one would willingly do that!). To accept either of these positions as pure fact would be to invite a cataclysm that would sweep us all away. And despite people in power who are dedicated to keeping us permanently afraid or to casually brushing aside the possibility of catastrophe, we have managed to survive and even thrive. Even twenty years ago, who would have believed the economic miracles that have taken place in India and China? So just as there are good and sufficient reasons to be afraid, there are plenty of reasons for us to believe in our future, collectively and as individuals. It would seem to be a matter of choice.

Fear and belief are emotions that we cannot get rid of but that we can learn to control. How? One way is to ground yourself relentlessly in reality. Yes, the problems of the world are enormous, even daunting. But will the sun come up tomorrow? Yes. For every step backward that we might take, there is just as good a reason to take one forward. One person losing a home to foreclosure is a personal disaster, but when it happens to enough people through no fault of their own, we rise as a collective group to do something about it. We change leaders, we review policies that haven't worked, we change them, we alter the way we do business, and we adjust our vision of reality to include new information. We don't bash our heads against a wall over and over in the hopes of getting a different outcome. We adapt. It's what we're good at. Or else we'd still be living in grass huts and praying to river-gods.

Somewhere back there in prehistory someone figured out that the tribe on the other side of the river had something that we needed, just as we had something they needed. The first to suggest trade was stoned to death for advocating contact with

Others (automatically the enemy). But eventually a few people sneaked across the river and came back with something of value. Then a few more people. Pretty soon the river's banks were filled with people working together and trading. Which won, fear or belief?

Assessing risk is something we all do. This can lead to fear, of course, but it can also throw light on problems. The wheel must have been achieved despite the fears some had that it might run somebody over. Both sides were right—the wheel made life better for many people, but some got run over. Does this mean we shouldn't use wheels? Hardly. But it does mean that we have to be careful with them, put safeguards in place, teach our children about the dangers of wheels, and build our roads and cities with those dangers in mind. Otherwise, we're back to walking. We cannot allow the fear of failure prevent us from trying new things. Trying new things is the only way we can improve on what has come before. Collective disaster, like individual disaster, is a call to try new things, like it or not. What was tried before led to this, so we'd better try something else since that didn't go so well (see hydrogen dirigibles, Hindenburg edition).

Dreaming of things unseen is something we all do, too. Even cynics dream. Putting those dreams into practice, however, leads to the problem of collaboration. Dreaming by oneself is not enough; others must share in it. So dreams must be communicated to others in such a way as to mobilize them to action. Recognizing this means that we can actually anticipate solutions to problems. Recognizing that we are not alone in facing these problems means that we can look to others' attempts at solutions with hope. Or we can look at how the problem we face was dealt with in the past and try that. The point is that without the belief in human ingenuity and human interconnectedness, no dream has any chance of succeeding. Benjamin Franklin, when facing the problem of a British invasion and a fractured Congress, advised that, "We must all hang together, or most assuredly we shall all hang separately." He might have been speaking to us today.

Belief need not be "starry-eyed" to be real and have real consequences. There is a collective belief in the existence and meaning of the life of Jesus Christ that has shaped our world for millennia. Is that "starry-eyed"? Religions all over the world depend on belief and faith as their bedrock. Are they "starry-eyed"? Cynics may deny the existence of God or abhor the practices of religion, but it is beyond dispute that religion has had a decisive impact on the way that people have organized the world. Does that make all the believers just "dreamers"? Consider the common humanity that is shared by people of different beliefs. Does the fact that people pray differently to different gods using different books as guides make them members of different species? No. But it does mean that people seek answers beyond their own senses, that people everywhere need to connect to others in ways that are not tangible, but that are important to them.

Neither fear nor belief is an answer. Both are signposts on the path to answers. Fear can be healthy or unhealthy, depending on what role you allow it to play in your life. Belief, too, can be healthy or unhealthy, and for the same reason. In order to tame these two viruses, though, and bring them under rational control, it is necessary to first understand them as what they are—necessary but not determinative. By themselves, neither is a perfect reflection of reality. Balanced against the collective desire for progress, fear is just a brake on advancement. Balanced against the collective dread of disaster, belief is just a big pair of rose-colored glasses. But balanced against each other, fear and belief can support and protect each other, guiding us to new solutions even as we are cautious about the possible pitfalls along the way. Together, they represent the extremes on the human spectrum, and like all extremes they cannot be overindulged. They can be harnessed, however, by a rational mind seeking moderation. It is in avoiding reality that these two get us into trouble. It is our responsibility, therefore, to account for both of these basic emotions only through the filter of reality.

Are there real reasons to fear? There certainly are, and anyone who claims to be entirely fearless is also letting you know that they are not rational. Are there good reasons to hope? There certainly are, as any pregnant woman can tell you. The future is within our grasp, and if we try to mold it properly, keeping the extremes at bay by reflecting on reality, then the future is certainly amenable to our hopes and plans for it.

Fear what you know is fearful, but don't fear what you don't know. Believe in yourself and in others, but not to the point where you cannot adjust to the setbacks and pitfalls that any new endeavor inevitably faces. The past is prologue, the future is unwritten. You have it in your power to write that future. What will guide you most? Fear, or belief?

"If the bar is too high, then you can use your tools of innovative ideas to build a ladder."

"THE DEPTHS OF DETERMINATION"
—DR. STEVEN M. HOEFFLIN

IT WAS NOT AN easy road that led to my success. Building one of the most highly regarded plastic surgery practices in the world was not just a road, but a roller coaster, complete with dozens of bumps, turns, and ups and downs.

Success is defined by the depth of your determination, the visualization of your victory, the intensity of your innovative ideas, your ability to act against adversity, and finally going all the way and grabbing your goal. There is story after story written about people with extraordinary challenges who reach the peak of success. Your own story is being written right now.

How did I achieve this success? It's not a very long story, but it is one I think you will find interesting.

First, a little history:

I was first in my family's history to go to college. I worked a full-time job and took full-time courses both in college and medical school. I ultimately graduated first in my medical school class at UCLA and received numerous awards. I went on to complete a full-time, sixteen-year education leading to my board certification in plastic and reconstructive surgery. I received the coveted Surgical Medal Award from Dr. William Longmire, the president of the American College of Surgeons.

During my forty-year medical career, I have had the honor of caring for over 50,000 patients from 126 different countries. My wonderful patients have spanned from a severely burned infant whom I kept alive, to an old homeless man whose amputated hand I successfully replanted, to performing cosmetic surgeries on world-famous kings, queens, and celebrities.

I also experienced a record number of challenges, obstacles, setups, and setbacks in pursuing my dream.

My decision to become a plastic surgeon came from a great mentor.

In my experience, almost every successful person that I have known has changed career goals one or even several times along the way.

During medical school, I actually wanted to be a heart surgeon. I participated in research involving different types of heart operations in calves. Heart surgery was extremely dramatic and interesting, but I had an artistic ability and yearned to be able to express this ability in surgery. When I graduated from medical school and started my surgical training, I became involved in research with Dr. Franklin Ashley. He was UCLA's chief of plastic surgery and was world-famous. I assisted him with numerous operations and I saw that this was an artistic endeavor and had immediate results. Through Dr. Ashley's great mentoring, I was introduced to another career goal. Although the training to be a plastic surgeon was two years longer than that for a general surgeon, my goal and dreams to be a plastic surgeon became a part of me.

It is these types of great experiences and mentoring that are so important in introducing various careers. From this type of introduction, visions, dreams, and goals are made and met.

This is why there is a tremendous benefit in exposing young children to as many different career options as possible through both direct experiences and at the direction of great mentors.

Where would our world be if Beethoven never saw or heard a piano, or if Einstein's uncle had never given him a magnetic compass? If one does not know what to do with their life, they should experience what many others are doing with their lives. These "career introductions" can act as motivators, guides, and pathways. Mentors are much more important than role models because they personally advise, instruct, and guide you. Our society, unfortunately, is losing the personal mentoring of children, and we will all suffer the creative loss.

When making difficult decisions, one cannot discount how prayer may clear and strengthen the head, heart, and soul. If one believes in a higher power, it gives you more power to believe in yourself. If one does not believe in a higher power, at least this is one's own personal belief. People can and do pray to themselves. What is tremendously important is that you always believe in yourself, your vision, your dreams, and your ultimate goal. People who have had it much tougher than you have made it, and have made it big, armed with nothing more than their belief in themselves.

There was a very important study done at Harvard on people who have had to make very difficult decisions. The study involved people who had great difficulty in choosing between two choices, say between A and B. I had a somewhat difficult choice between heart surgery and plastic surgery. When they studied these people ten years later, whether someone had chosen A or B, the outcome was about the same. But what was both surprising and crystal clear was the following: Even if you have difficulty choosing between A and B, the ultimate outcome will be almost the same.

Intelligent people who weigh the positives and negatives between two choices, and then have difficulty making a choice, usually have choices that are really nearly equal.

Otherwise these choices wouldn't be so difficult. But what really stands out as a serious problem is when one fails to make a decision at all.

In my forty-year medical career, I have trained over 1,000 physicians, medical students, nurses, and other types of health care professionals. I have told many of them about this study and I do not remember anyone telling me that they ultimately made the wrong choice. I do remember too many to count who could not make a decision. Most of them lost their dream and really ended up getting their third choice, which was no choice.

I've never seen hard work hurt anyone's chances of being successful. Hard work just makes it harder to fail.

Many people think that training to be a doctor is like surviving a seesaw of suffering. Well, they are right. But when you are finished training to be a doctor, training to be a surgeon is truly much harder.

Everyone knows that the training to become a physician, no less a surgeon, is one of the most rigorous career paths one can take. It is exponentially harder than U.S. Marine Corps boot camp. Boot camp is six weeks. Surgical training is six grueling years of twenty-four-seven training. I attended UCLA for medical school, my surgical residency, and my plastic surgery residency. This entire process took twenty-six years to complete: twelve years of grammar and high school, four years of college, four years of medical school, four years of surgical residency, and an additional two years of plastic surgery residency. Then you start all over again by going out into private practice.

UCLA Medical Center has one of the best and most demanding surgical training programs in the country. It is extremely difficult to enter the program, and they only accept twenty of the best medical students from around the country who graduate in the top ten percent of their class. Through the entire process, the twenty first-year surgical residents would be, let's say, "carved down" over the next five years to two of the "best" residents, who would eventually become the "chief residents" of the program.

The days often started at 5:15 a.m. and lasted until midnight. The schedule repeated itself for the next six years. You stayed up all night every other day and had to learn the art of catnapping. Every morning, there was a team of up to fourteen health care professionals who would make "rounds" to check on as many as sixty hospitalized surgical patients before going to the operating room at 7:30 a.m. This team would usually be led by one of the surgical professors.

My first day as a surgical resident was one of the most memorable days of my surgical training. With this type of experience, you find out that to be a good surgeon requires more than just hard work. You have to become a fervent disciple of discipline.

That morning, the chief of the department of surgery, Dr. William Longmire, was leading the "rounds." He had a celebrity patient in the intensive care unit who had a very long and difficult operation due to cancer of the bile duct. This required making a long incision in the abdomen and chest. At the end of the operation, a chest tube was inserted in order to drain air and fluid from the lungs. Due to the complexity of this surgery, the tube had to be removed by a more experienced third-year resident, not a first-year surgical resident. He asked the resident to come in at 4 a.m. and arrange an X-ray, check the X-ray results to make sure the fluid was gone, remove the chest tube, and take another X-ray to ensure that the lungs were fully expanded. To leave the ICU, the patient had to be free of any chest tube. To leave it in too long could cause a life-threatening infection.

The next day, we gathered at 5:15 a.m. in the ICU for rounds. As I entered the room, I saw that the chest tube was still in the patient and the third-year surgical resident looked like a ghost. When the professor saw this, he walked over to the resident and asked him what had happened. The resident told the professor that he had forgotten to do what he had asked of him as he never got to bed. This was not a good excuse, as no one slept on many nights and absolutely no one ever forgets a direct order from the professor. On the way out of the ICU, the professor shook the resident's hand and said, "I hope you have a better memory in your next residency program." With that, the professor fired the resident on the spot.

In the military, if you disobey a direct order from a superior, you get court-martialed. If you disobey a direct order from the professor, and jeopardize a patient, you can lose your surgical residency.

This experience was a very important milestone for me and everyone else. In surgical training, ten percent of the job is performing the operation while the other ninety percent is keeping your patient safe and out of trouble. This is how surgeons are trained and this is how they fall out of the training program if they unnecessarily jeopardize a patient. One mistake can cost a patient his or her life.

What were the lessons that I learned that I could share with you?

You need to work hard to be successful. But you also need much more. You have to constantly focus and visualize where you are going and what you need to do each and every day. In your mind, you can visualize your goals. But, with your eyes, you must look down and watch every step. You are really your own competition. This resident could have easily written himself a note to remind him of his obligation. I have never really seen a successful person who does not make notes to him or herself.

You will always do right if you choose to do what's right. Almost everyone knows the right thing to do, but many choose not to do it. This third-year resident could have called another surgical resident to do the important task if he was too sleepy. This would have been the right thing to do.

I learned that as a surgeon you are responsible for the safety and welfare of your patients and must always do what is right every time. As in so many things in life, when other lives are at stake, this type of decision is not yours. There is no choice here between, say, A or B. There is one and only one decision: You do the right thing or you find someone else to do the right thing for you. When people's lives and welfare are at stake, you can never do the wrong thing. You will never get away with it, and certainly those whom you are responsible for will not, either.

In more than three decades since I entered private practice, I have seen innumerable people fail to reach their goals because they knew the right thing to do but chose not to do it.

One of the most important ingredients to one's success is very frequently overlooked by goal-oriented individuals. This is the creation of innovative ideas to help you reach your goal and beyond. If the bar is too high, then you can use your tools of innovative ideas to build a ladder.

I vividly remember two great innovative ideas that I learned while observing my beautiful mother:

"You're wise to rise early."

"You can multitask on the go."

I have used these two ideas continually throughout my life. They are a powerful springboard to success.

I was raised in a very poor area on South Hobart Street in Los Angeles. I grew up with four brothers, all about a year apart. As my mother had five young boys, how would she keep us in order and still do the things that she needed to do for all of us and herself?

Every day, she would get up very early when everyone else was asleep. She would complete all of her housework in a fraction of the time that she could ever do during a regular day. My father was always amazed at her efficiency.

Like my mother, ever since I entered high school, I would train myself to get up at 4:30 a.m. and do all my studying and busywork before school. I would have never received A's in school or graduated first in my class at UCLA if I did not follow this plan. It was very difficult at first, but it worked for me and I still do it to this day.

A mother with five young boys can babysit and do many things by just using one word: streetcar. A few times a week, our mother would walk us one block to the streetcar stop. We would hop on and sit in the back. We would go around and around the city for hours. All of my brothers and I were fascinated and mesmerized by what we saw out of the windows, the clanking of the streetcar, and the other passengers.

My mother would sit, knit, read books, visit with or teach us, write letters, and many other things. She had prepared sandwiches and little containers of milk for us in a paper bag. Before she left, she would often call and invite some of her friends to hop on board for a nice visit with her. This was the true definition of "multitasking on the go." To this day, I terribly miss her and the clanging of the streetcars.

Coming up with innovative ideas from your mind is like a miner coming up with a handful of gold from his gold mine. You have to dig and dig and never give up. I have found it useful to identify something that doesn't work for me or something that is stopping me from progressing. Then you try to come up with as many simple methods that you can think of to resolve this challenge. One will stand out and then you should try it and develop it to help you reach your goal and the gold. Remember, inspiration is the amount of interest that you put into creating your innovative ideas.

I had great difficulty in trying to work enough hours to afford school and to study at the same time. At age sixteen, I started working as a box boy at Hughes Market every Saturday and Sunday. I was paid $1.25 per hour. To meet expenses in college, I worked every weekend and some evenings. As expenses escalated, so did the hours I worked and the number of college classes I had to attend. In both college and medical school, I essentially worked a full-time job on the weekends and evenings and then attended classes during the day.

I had to learn to study "on the go." I could not carry books to study while I was working. So I developed my memory to retain the large number of facts and numbers I had to contend with every day. I patterned this after the technique that savants use to have such striking memories.

I now call it GPS. This stands for "Great Pictures and Stories." Geniuses remember large amounts of facts and numbers. It turns out that savants (like Dustin Hoffman's character in *Rain Man*) use the same memory technique but don't realize it.

In order to remember things forward, backward, and upside-down, I created the GPS technique of memory stickers and the handless clocks. I have developed hundreds and hundreds of these techniques. I would get up very early and study. I would commit the facts and numbers that I needed to know into these types of "photographic memories." During the day, when I was working or walking, I would remember these facts and review them in my head. I would multitask, I would study on the go, and so can you!

If you think you have had a lot of challenges that have knocked you down or knocked you out, just come knocking at my door and I will tell you my story!

Some of the challenges facing you can appear to be an insurmountable Mount Everest. You can and will prevail, despite the magnitude of the challenge facing you. In 1975, while I was still a plastic surgery resident at the UCLA Hospital Medical Center, my second son, Brad, was born. At first, something didn't seem right to the pediatricians. Brad was hospitalized several times at the Los Angeles Children's Hospital. I was told that he had an unexpected brain enzyme disorder and another as-yet-undefined neurological problem. At four months, when he was not developing, we were told that Brad would never walk or talk and would have to be institutionalized for his entire life. This was totally devastating to me. As I dealt with all of this, my wife was unable to cope, left me, and filed for divorce.

That evening, I was on call at a reconstructive hospital for neurologically injured patients (Rancho Los Amigos Hospital in the Los Angeles area). As was customary for on-call doctors, I was assigned to sleeping in the old military barracks near the hospital. I was in a small room with a cot and a single lightbulb hanging from the ceiling. I just put my head into my hands and started to cry. At that moment, I promised myself that I would do anything in my power to keep Brad out of an institution and to help him. I needed to persist in this quest and have a lot of patience to see it happen.

Despite my 100-hour workweek at UCLA, I found additional work as an emergency room doctor on my rare free evenings and weekends to meet the extra expenses. I was now a single father and I had a son who really needed me. None of the physicians could determine why he was not thriving. His neurological condition worsened.

I just persisted and had patience that the answer would come to us and he would be helped. I took Brad from specialist to specialist without any helpful diagnosis or treatment plan being offered. As the experts were no help, I kept on digging and searching for answers. Despite dozens of doctor visits over several years, no diagnosis was established and Brad never improved. Finally, when Brad was seventeen, I met a brilliant neurologist, Dr. Michael Gold, who was suspicious that Brad's nerve disorder might be a disorder of the covering of his nerves, which is called myelin. Without the myelin covering, his nerves were "short-circuiting," which was the cause of his paralysis. His neurological disorder was called CIPD (chronic inflammatory demyelinating polyneuropathy). There was a new experimental treatment called IVIG that could help Brad, but due to its scarcity, the drug cost about $20,000 a month. I got another mortgage on my house, worked four jobs, and gave Dr.

Gold the green light to start this treatment. Miraculously, Brad started improving. He started walking better, had less pain, and started to gain weight. Given the previous diagnosis by the other doctors, this was nothing short of a miracle.

One has no other choice but to persist and have patience when facing the enormous challenges of being responsible for a child's life. In my early career, I saved hundreds of severely injured and burned children as the result of this experience with my own son.

When we were growing up in our South Los Angeles neighborhood, there was a large population of "hobos" (which was the term for the homeless at the time) who would go door-to-door to beg for food and clothing. My mother was an easy mark and they seemed to come just to our house. They also took advantage of her by coming back more than once a day. They even tried to steal things from around the house. My mother told me that the hobos in the neighborhood would secretly place a hidden "mark" on a house to show that the family inside is a family that will give food and clothing to hobos when asked.

On numerous occasions, despite my being a "nice guy," I have been the target of attacks, burglars, con men, divorce and infidelity, death threats, embezzlers, frauds, gangs, hucksters, etc. I even had my own long-term employees steal, attempt to extort money, and fabricate stories about me.

In the early 1990s, several ex-employees and two doctors, who had all worked for me for many years, attempted to extort a large amount of money from me. Together with several attorneys, they concocted an unbelievable story that I was mocking and photographing celebrities who were in my surgical facility while they were under general anesthesia. This fabricated story was picked up by the press and went all over the world. They slandered, defamed, and tried to embarrass me. This was the most emotionally difficult and heart-wrenching challenge that I have ever had to face. As there was not a word of truth in the allegations, I persisted and had patience in the hard work that it took to clear my name. I also sued all of them and won big apologies and large settlements. My efforts to regain my reputation with my patients, family, and friends started with calling, apologizing, and ensuring my patients that what was being claimed never happened. I was extremely worried and embarrassed just walking down the street. I was a very well-known plastic surgeon and wondered what people were thinking. Over two-thirds of the people walking the street are dealing with their own major challenges in life. The other third are just waiting for their problem to show up. Many people face terrible problems such as a malignancy, bankruptcy, or the death of an immediate family member.

I had to muster every particle of determination to endure and prevail over these serious challenges. All of our lives go through continuous cycles. We have sunny days when everything is going very well. Then we have winter days when we have to face these terrible and dark challenges. We have to expect the dark days in our lives and act like a squirrel storing nuts for the winter. We need to create an "emotional reserve"—that reserve is knowing that you have your own "formula" tucked away for the bad days ahead.

If it weren't for my persistence and patience in fighting these many kinds of mischief and malfeasance, I would probably have given up a long time ago and not continued to pursue the dreams and goals of my life.

These are the two "legs" that will carry your legacy. Our real purpose in life is to create something great and then contribute it to others. One great contribution is creating children who will carry on your legacy, the creation of wonderful music or books, or creating an innovative invention or a great company. When one fertilizes his or her creativity, it will grow into a large tree of knowledge that can distribute untold quantities of fruitful opportunities to others.

I was blessed with the opportunity to create 200 scientific manuscripts, several books, numerous new and unique plastic and reconstructive surgical techniques, and new types of instruments. My contribution was teaching this new knowledge to plastic surgeons through lectures, seminars, and surgeries in eighty-two countries. Two of my favorite works stand out. I created the first mathematical definition of beautiful faces and published a book called *The Beautiful Face*. I also wrote a breakthrough paper entitled "23,000 Consecutive General Anesthetics with No Serious Complications." I wrote dozens of innovative ideas that provided patients with a very safe operating room environment and anesthesia. This became a standard for many plastic surgeons.

A medical practice is the only business where trade secrets are freely shared with your competitors. Freely teaching others is a physician's obligation, and it actually teaches you new thoughts and elevates your own success. I am very much opposed to patenting new treatments or operations, like many of my colleagues have attempted to do.

For thirty years, I served on the board of directors or as a president of numerous societies and hospital divisions. I have been awarded several prestigious teaching awards. Thirty-six years ago, as the result of my younger son's severe neurological disabilities, I developed numerous unique and innovative learning programs. As a single father, I homeschooled him in these techniques and he excelled. I then shared these techniques with other families who had children with serious learning disorders.

Recently I have been focusing my efforts on child humanitarian projects. For example, I created a technique to easily eradicate landmines—which was presented to Nelson Mandela at the World Landmine Conference in 2006—by using simple dried mud balls that can be thrown to clear a marked path in a field of mines. Currently, I am publishing a book and animated DVD series entitled *Learn How to Learn, Think How to Think*. My wife, Pamela, and I support an orphanage in Acapulco and we are planning on using innovative ideas to improve the largest shantytown of impoverished children in Latin America.

You can have great success if you find a career that is a dream for you. A career choice comes more easily through a mentor introduction or by introducing yourself to a wide range of experiences and career possibilities. There are three rules and routes to great success that you must always follow. These are hard work, creating innovative ideas to help you climb your ladder to success, and the persistence and patience to get there. One of the greatest rewards of success is the ability to take your creation and contribute it to others.

Despite the many opportunities I have had to directly help people with life-threatening illnesses, the ability to teach these techniques to others has been even more rewarding. Knowing that my effort, my sacrifice, and my persistence helped pave the way for others to avoid the pitfalls that I have experienced has put all the problems and difficulties I have faced in perspective. Knowing what can be survived and overcome has made it easier for me to advance my goals in life. Knowing that survival has been crucial for the others in my life has helped me, too. I know that we all face setbacks and catastrophes—I am here to tell you that if I can overcome them, so can you!

**“Without vision, nothing is possible.
With vision, nothing is impossible.”**

THE GIFT OF VISION

WHAT IS VISION? What does vision do? Why is it necessary? How can you acquire vision? Generations of inventors, scientists, researchers, investors, and others engaged in carving out the future have been asked the same question: What are you doing? This question is followed by an even more unanswerable one: Why? For most people, it is far simpler to ask why something should be done, rather than nothing. Just as young children find it inconceivable that there can be two names for one thing, so as we get older we hang on more and more tightly to the things we know for sure. Rather than take a chance on a new idea, we cling to the past and refuse to exercise the one human quality that has lifted us out of a state of pure nature and into progress. One of the early heads of the U.S. Patent Office resigned in the 1830s on the grounds that everything that could be invented had already been invented. This is an extreme example of the principle, but the simple truth remains: for those without vision, the world is a very limited place.

Vision is one's personal goal. Vision is the absolute prerequisite for hope. Vision not only illuminates the future;

once you have accepted your own vision of your own life, the past comes into sharp relief, too. Without vision, nothing is possible. With vision, nothing is impossible. Imagine a world without television, without radio, without computers, without spaceflight, or satellites, or microwaves, or cell phones—to cite just a few very recent advancements. In short, imagine the world of our grandparents. If you had told them that measles, chicken pox, and malaria no longer killed huge numbers of Americans, the best they could probably have imagined was that God had lifted these scourges from the Earth. Imagine what they would have thought about the possibilities we dream of today. If no visionary had been allowed to put his ideas into practice, what would we be?

You obtain power, you operate in love, and you engage in self-discipline only after you discover your vision. The power of sight is meaningless without vision. As the old saying goes, eyes that look are common, but eyes that see are rare. Can you think of a single worthwhile or noble thing that was ever accomplished without the inspiring power of someone's vision? If Einstein had not challenged Newton—that is, if he had not taken another look at what-everyone-knew-for-sure—would we have the modern world? Doubtful. Yet while he was working on his ideas he was just a patent clerk, someone whose doodling could have been dismissed as the scratches of a failed math teacher. Today? We have been to the moon, we have photographed atoms, and we have seen the center of the galaxy.

Mankind's evolution is permeated with examples of the creative and tradition-defying visions of truly independent thinkers. Every single original thing and its advancement in the economic, medical, political, and social world is the direct result of the power of vision. Vision is the essential thing that propels us from what we are to what we can become. Vision can break the chains of limitations that we call reality, and it permits us to cross over into the liberty of what we think we can be. Vision brings the unseen to life and the unknown into reality. A true visionary can endure disappointment, despair, and tribulation because he sees what can be accomplished. Vision inspires the discouraged and motivates the exasperated. Vision is the bedrock of courage and the fuel of perseverance; it is the energy of progress and prosperity.

While some visionaries make great contributions that affect masses of people, many others have no vision for their own lives and are doomed to suffer the consequences. Still others have a vision but no clue about how to make it real. Of course, there are also those with a vision who have abandoned their dreams and aspirations after setbacks or frustrations. There isn't a single individual who has contributed to this book, nor any person who has transformed his life, who has not encountered more obstacles than any set of volumes can document. The difference between those who have succeeded and those who have not—besides perseverance—is their ability to accurately define their vision, to capture that vision, and to allow no one else to redefine their vision for them. They understood that their vision depended on matching their actions to an internal reality only they could see. Their vision was the critical link to their destiny. Their future was not ahead of them, but within them.

The tragic fact of our reality is that our lives do not accurately reflect what we are capable of becoming. I've spent nearly two decades writing about people in one format or another. Since I was twelve years old, I've had an insatiable desire to know what makes people tick. Of course, there was a motivating factor: I desperately wanted to change my own reality.

My reality was not good. When I was a first-grader in Yugoslavia, the school nurse marked every vertebra on my back with a marker as I bent over during a physical. When I straightened, the marks on my back showed an abnormal curvature of the spine. Four years after coming to America, when my family and I were living in Chicago, my mother brought to my father's attention the fact that my right shoulder blade was protruding—the deformity had become visible to the naked eye.

Within a week my father took me to the doctor, and within days after that I was wrapped in a full-body cast at Chicago's Columbia Hospital, awaiting a radical surgery for a forty-five-degree spinal curve.

A month later a steel rod was placed into my spine. Each month after that, I had the cast removed and was stretched on a machine. (In the Middle Ages they called this "the rack," and it was not used for medical treatment but for torture). A new cast was then wrapped around my entire body, except for my arms and legs. I remained in bed for six months, without any physical therapy. I wasn't allowed to get myself up and begin learning to walk again for another six months, and then only with a "walking body cast." Of course, my muscles had atrophied, and it took months before I could make it from one end of the apartment to the other on my own. The pain was excruciating.

Morphine shots eased the physical suffering, but there was a mental anguish that wasn't assuaged by drugs. The evening prior to my surgery, I overheard my father and the orthopedic surgeon talking in the quiet corridor outside my room. The doctor reminded my father that the procedure was not foolproof, that there was a possibility that multiple surgeries would be required over the years, and that complications such as partial paralysis could not be ruled out.

I heard my father reply in a very stern voice that there would be no complications. It sounded like a threat. After that, all went silent. Years later, my father told me that he spent hours that snow-filled December night just aimlessly driving through the streets, weeping.

I remained flat on my back. I couldn't lift my head because the cast went up to my jawbone and to the top of my head in the back. I couldn't sit up because it went below my hip bones. There was no television and I could not lift my arms to read a book. I was a frightful sight, so few children came to visit. I observed the changing of the seasons by the tree that reached the window of our third-story apartment. I had two options: the radio, and thinking.

To tell you the truth, the anguish on my parents' faces was far worse than the pain and loneliness of my situation. I knew how hard my father had to work and how hopeless my mother felt. My brother was sent off to the Gilmour Academy, a Catholic boys' boarding school outside Cleveland.

With nothing but time on my hands, I reviewed the entire course of my life and mapped out my entire future. I stubbornly refused to accept any limitations and was determined to make a full recovery. When a wheelchair was brought to me six months into the ordeal, something violent stirred within me. I went into a rage. I saw that wheelchair as a symbol of defeat, and I was *not* going to go there! It was quickly whisked away, never to be brought back. During this "thinking" period I realized that my position in the socioeconomic pecking order was not an enviable one; it offered very few favors and virtually no possibility of escape. By all accounts it was a frightfully limiting environment. I knew there was more out there. While I understood that I was well beyond where I had come from, I was also painfully aware that I was far behind where I wanted to be.

I reasoned that education was the way out; reading became my salvation. I considered every possible career opportunity and racked my brain trying to come up with a profession that would help me escape and a career that would give me opportunities to expand the scope of my environment. I wanted grand adventures and I wanted to meet all kinds of people. I wanted to have an option-filled life, and, of course, I wanted to make a lot of money. From early childhood, I understood that economic power meant personal freedom.

Later, with my much-improved physical and mental posture, I set out to become a journalist. A year after that, I began to write. In addition, I began to do two to three hours of aerobics every day. Somewhat like Forrest Gump, I began to walk, and I've kept the routine of walking six to ten miles per day to the present. I never suffered any back complications, and although my personal and professional journey took more twists and turns than the road from Maui to Hana, I have not only managed to fulfill my goals, but I have exceeded them beyond my greatest expectations. Needless to say, once you realize that you can create your future, the goal-setting process eventually goes into orbit—you begin to challenge yourself in ways that most mortals would not deem sane, let alone remotely possible.

The beginning of any new enterprise, whether a business or the reinvention of your life, requires something that is indispensable: a leap of faith. Faith, like vision, is the substance of things hoped for; it is what you can see that others cannot. Faith has been known to overcome the most enormous impediments, to make the wildest things possible, and to literally move mountains. The very day I understood that I had access to this most powerful human quality, I began to use it. The results have been nothing less than miraculous—yet I did nothing that had not been done by many others before me. I simply activated myself. I stopped thinking about the problems I would have accomplishing goals and began to think of ways around the problems. Faith did not solve anything, but it did give me the necessary precondition to resolution—it gave me hope. Once I had that, I knew that nothing—not ignorance, not superstition, not cynicism, not so-called expertise, nothing but nothing—could stop me.

Once I came to this realization, well, to call it liberating would be a gross understatement. I felt a new freedom that I had never imagined possible. I could write my own ticket to the future. I was bound by nothing, and so could be stopped by nothing.

Some years ago I ran across an illuminating story about Walt Disney. Its inspiring message has never left me. It has been noted that a visionary's vision is his reality. For few others in history has this been more true than for Walt Disney. When Disney World opened in 1971 with its relatively few rides, he was seen sitting on a bench in the theme park and staring into space. A groundskeeper approached him and asked, "How are you, sir?" Without taking much notice of his employee, Disney replied, "Fine." He continued staring into space.

The groundskeeper grew concerned. "Sir, what are you doing?" he asked. Disney replied, "I'm looking at my mountain. I see the mountain *right there*."

Disney conveyed his vision from that bench to the architects. While the crew went to work, Walt Disney died. At the dedication ceremony of Space Mountain, the speaker who introduced Mrs. Disney said, "It's a pity that Mr. Walt Disney is not here today to see his mountain. But we are glad his wife is here." Mrs. Disney then took her place at the podium and said to the crowd, "Walt already saw the mountain. It is *you* who are now seeing it for the first time."

Whether it is Bill Gates, who left Harvard after one semester to pursue his vision, or the guy who ditched school and went on to start FedEx after an economics professor wrote, "Do not dream of things that cannot happen" across his essay—visionaries cannot be shrinking violets. They must be true to themselves, despite naysayers and cynics and all the people who are quick to call something "impossible." History echoes with the outraged cries of those who yelled, "Impossible!" And history is littered with their forgotten cries. Think of all the people in your life who have spent time and energy trying to convince you of all the things you couldn't do, all the things you could never have, all the things that they are sure cannot be accomplished. Is it a long list? Almost all of us have faced these people and their negative messages. Many of us have given up trying; how can you defeat all the naysayers? There are so many of them. How do you defeat them? How do you overcome the people who see the world as finished, complete, immutable? It takes faith and it takes vision. Often you must maintain the two in the face of determined opposition. That is the job of self-discipline—to recognize the fear that limits other people, yet maintain your faith in the face of it.

To transform your life is not easy, but if you have faith in your ultimate success, the task becomes not only not impossible, but a positive pleasure. Activating yourself so you can reach your potential is not the story of Sisyphus, doomed to push the rock up the hill in vain, but the story of Noah, whose faith was ultimately rewarded more greatly than he could have dreamed. A man of faith was granted a vision, and despite the protests and obstructions of his neighbors, he kept his faith and was saved from devastation and extinction. We are all his children; shouldn't we embrace his example?

“Fortune favors the prepared mind.”

"WE ARE ENDLESSLY POSSIBLE" —PAUL ANKA

I'VE BEEN VERY lucky. I was lucky to have amazing parents who supported me from an early age in everything I did. I was lucky to grow up at a time and in a place that rewarded hard work and talent. I was lucky to have met the people that I did at the times that I met them. I was very lucky to have been as successful as I was by the time I was twenty-two, much less everything else I've been blessed with. But as the man said, "Fortune favors the prepared mind." I was lucky, but I also knew that I could never count on that. It wasn't something that, in and of itself, would put any food on the table. I was lucky, true. But I also knew that in order for that to mean anything, I had to work as hard as I could to get the most out of it that I could.

From the time I was young, I enjoyed a kind of success that is given to very few people today. I was a teen heartthrob in the 1950s, not too long after Elvis Presley. I was a little different from most of the heartthrobs in that I wrote my own music. This gave me a confidence in myself that I have been very grateful for over the years. I've seen many others who came and went because they were essentially artists whose appeal was visual. I knew I could write music, and I knew that writing counted. In fact, I understood even when I was being mobbed in public that my heartthrob image wouldn't last. From the earliest time I can remember, I was always trying to look around the next corner, trying to figure out the next place where I needed to be. I didn't let myself get too satisfied. There were too many examples of the consequences of that, and I didn't want to end up as one more. How many ex-heartthrobs are out there? Too many. Before I was twenty-one, I knew that my career as a heartthrob was over. Fortunately, I had things to fall back on. I always tried to keep my options open, and ever since I have advised people to do the same. Don't close yourself off from the rest of the world just because you happen to be good at one aspect of it. That's death to the imagination. Test yourself. Try different arenas. Don't be afraid of change. Change is the only thing we can count on happening. In the world of music, it's easy to recognize this. I have had many fans over many years tell me "I remember you whenever..." and I've always been grateful that I did not stay in the picture frame of their memories. Many artists over the years have been relegated to that special place in their fans' minds—a particular time and place and age when they were young—and that's where they live: in memories. People don't have any idea that those young artists are gone now because they could not change, they could not adapt. In music, popularity is almost always temporary, no matter how big it is. It's a little like watching evolution on fast-forward: things change so fast that it's impossible to register one new species before the next one becomes the phenomenon of the day.

I changed. I made a conscious transition from trying to be the greatest heartthrob in the world to expanding my possibilities. I wrote the theme to the film *The Longest Day* in 1962 (acted in it, too). I worked in nightclubs, Las Vegas, and other venues. I was lucky, but I was also keeping an eye on the future. I knew that whatever I was doing at the time to keep myself busy and active, the most important thing I was doing was writing. I understood that writing would give me the most independence, the most freedom. If I wrote my own songs, I could write the plan for my own life.

This may not be something everyone can do, but I'm amazed sometimes by the simple fact that many people have talents that they don't cultivate. If you have a talent—at anything—then it seems to me that it's your responsibility to take advantage of that talent, to try to make something of it. So many people seem to settle for their lives rather than explore the possibilities that are contained in them. I don't understand anyone who is complacent, who sits down and says: "Okay, I'm good at this; I'm sticking with this *and nothing else!"* What's the point of that? Self-satisfaction? A willingness to be bored? Why do people do it to themselves? People seem to want to achieve a certain level of comfort and then lock themselves into it, without variation, without growth, and ultimately without hope of retaining those lives. Because however permanent you think the world is, it's not. Whatever is the foundation of your dream life, it's going to change. If you get too comfortable, something will come along to pull your chair out from under you. No one is immune to the effects of life, and its changes are more wrenching and brutal for those who believe it will always be the same, that nothing will ever change.

I was always conscious of not being put in a box. These days, with people bombarded all day, every day with images on television telling them what to look like, what to want, and what to buy, it seems that no one can avoid the box they are put into, no matter what they do. I believe that you must see the nature of the box you are in before you can do anything about getting out of it. Once you realize that you are caged, you have to do everything possible to escape. You have to gain control over your life before you can properly start to live it. And you cannot gain control of it until you look at yourself honestly. Have I done all that I could? Have I truly taken advantage of my opportunities? I tried very hard all my life to explore every new possibility that came my way. They didn't always work out, but the search always yielded something important for me—a new song, a new venue, partnership with a new artist, an innovation, an adaptation. There was always something useful, and often very valuable, that came from embracing the changes. Little was ever gained living in the past.

It's important to take stock of your environment. Look around you. Notice what other people are doing. If you see someone who is successful at something, ask yourself what that person is doing right. It seems easier and easier for people to feel entitled to be resentful or envious when they see someone famous. Why? Why not use it as a springboard instead of a measuring tape? Why must one person's success come at the expense of another's? There is nothing written that says that it is required for success to come at someone else's expense. I've never believed that. I have lived my life not believing that and actively working against it. It has been as important to me to promote the work of other people as it has been to promote myself. Credit is something you can only really give to yourself.

That's another thing people have lost as they have become more and more media-driven: the ability to accurately judge themselves and give themselves the credit they deserve. Why do people need to hear what others think about them before they make up their minds? The media have never been more important in promoting this myth of fame.

I talk to young people who openly tell me they want to be famous. I ask them, "Okay, what do you want to do?" Blank stare. Then, "I don't know." What's more disturbing is that often they don't even *care* what they're famous for; fame is the whole goal. Ironically, politicians never proclaim outright that they are ambitious. Yet they are the ones who really *are* ambitious. They're the ones who really *need* to be ambitious, yet we have become so hypocritical that they cannot say what many untalented, unimaginative, and uncreative people have no problem announcing to the world. How did that happen? When will we shake the illusions of fame and begin to appreciate the real heroes and icons around us? I've never understood why pop stars get the attention they do. It's only a temporary job, at best. No real job security without talent and effort—like most jobs worth doing. Still, applicants line the blocks of every city and town. "Who wants to be a [fill in the blank]?" Everyone, it seems. Why? Blank stares all around. Needing someone *else* to tell you that you have talent, that you are worthy, has become a disease, one capable of destroying personalities, families, and individuals.

There are other consequences to this reliance on external validation. People stop relying on themselves; they chase others' opinions; they close themselves off from the greatest source of satisfaction that everyone has—their own freedom. Some people take for granted what they have. They don't realize that most people in the world can't even begin to dream of the things that they already have and *are dissatisfied with*. With the TV on everywhere, it's easy to understand why people are so dissatisfied. They are being shown images of exotic places that seem so much more glamorous than what they experience. It's impossible that they won't want those things, those places, those luxuries that they are being shown every day. The dream of success dies hard, but in this media-driven world, it is not driven by achievement in reality, but simply by fame. And fame that doesn't have to be about anything. This is wrong, and it can be scary. People need to be able to feel good about themselves, and as long as they don't hurt anyone else in pursuing this happiness, they should be allowed to do what they want and be who they want. But too many people don't believe in themselves enough to pursue that happiness. The images on TV seduce them into thinking that if only they were on TV they could be *as famous as* [fill in the blank]. But by relying on what they *see*, they ignore how they *feel*. And once that process begins, people think the only way they can *be* somebody is if others recognize them as someone worth *being like*.

This skips most of the steps required to have actual feelings about real things, instead of impulses about pictures coming out of a box. They call that dehumanization, and for good reason.

Something can be done about being stuck in a box, or hooked to a box, or hooked on a box. Once you see the nature of the cage you're in, you can turn your energy and concentration to the problem of getting out. History shows that once people are motivated to solve a problem, they almost always find a way to do it. When I think of how the world has changed in the last fifty years, my mind reels. Fifty years ago we were all stunned by Sputnik. Remember Sputnik? The first satellite? Launched by the Soviet Union? Right. Now saying the words "satellite" and "Soviet Union" together seems not just quaint, but strange. Most people would think of these things and draw a blank. But in their day, they were both earthquakes that shook history. Who knows what earthquake will come next? I do know that it's better to embrace change than fear it. If we know that things are going to change, and that those changes are going to profoundly affect us, shouldn't we prepare for it?

As an entertainer I always understood that you could never rest on yesterday's accomplishments. The show must go on, and so must I. I've always looked for opportunities to do more and different things. I could never be satisfied just doing the same things over and over. I have traveled the world and I have been startled to find that, as different as people might be, it is their similarities that keep cropping up. Over and over I have found that people all want safety and security for their families, a solid environment for their children, and the fulfillment of their dreams. But they are not all one way or the other. They all adapt to their circumstances, they all change—like it or not. The ones I have known who have been the most successful are the ones who take this principle to heart.

These people are the ones who not only adapt to change, but seek it. They are often the change agents, the ones who bring on a more general, more popular change. I've written many songs, and performed many, too, but I was not always the best interpreter of my own work. I understood this from an early age, and I also learned that the best result can come from letting someone else interpret your work. This isn't just true of songwriting. There are many, many talented and creative people who are invisible to the public. It's not that they don't get credit or compensation for their work, its' just that their work doesn't require their physical presence. Many working people experience this, but instead of satisfaction they feel unrecognized. Why? Because the only recognition they can accept is fame. People work hard at important jobs all their lives and what do they remember most? The time they were on TV for some reason or another, something not related to the very real and significant roles they play every day. Not everyone works in a field where they can hand off their work to make someone else famous, true. But isn't it just as important that people learn to be satisfied with the real contributions they do make? Feeding children, fighting fires, running a business to support a family, working hard at school—these are things worthy of recognition and respect. Fame comes and goes; true accomplishment lives forever.

I have not planted my flag yet. There are many more mountains to climb. I believe that we are endlessly possible. That is, we can be who we want if we just will it. For as many problems as there are in the world today, there are that many possibilities, too. I feel that about my own future, and I've been working nonstop since I was sixteen years old. I have been unusually fortunate, I know. I also know that good fortune by itself is not enough. If more people seized their own potential, they would find not only a greater source of happiness than can be found in fame, but also an enduring way to live their lives happily. Isn't that the best thing, after all? Isn't that what we all seek? Are there any other answers out there but the ones we've always known—love, hope, effort, achievement? If there are, I would love to know them. But until someone comes up with new answers to replace the old ones, I'll stick with those. They've worked pretty well so far.

“The words of a man’s mouth are as deep waters.”

Bernie Brillstein was among the first to enthusiastically come on board to be a part of this book. At the time, it was not a first person format, hence the difference in style. Sadly, Bernie passed away just before we went to press. He is dearly missed by all of us who loved and appreciated him. I am grateful to his wife, Carrie, for her assistance in our endeavors. Bernie was the epitome of what "life transformation" stands for. He not only miraculously transformed his own life, but the lives of virtually everyone who joined forces with him. It was his wish that his journey may inspire you as well.

"I REALLY CONDUCTED WARFARE WONDERFULLY!" —BERNIE BRILLSTEIN

"I'M ENJOYING MY LEGENDRY," Bernie Brillstein said quietly—looking like the cat that swallowed the canary—at the end of several meetings on a bright and sunny Beverly Hills afternoon. After more than half a century as an entertainment industry behind-the-scenes icon in the badlands of Hollywood, the seventy-six-year-old power broker remained a five-star general among its troops until the day he died.

Bernie Brillstein was an unrivaled leader in the world of show business. He was a top packager and producer, a devastatingly successful personal manager, and a most-sought-after consultant. He reinvented a vital aspect of the business that no one has been able to duplicate to this day. As the founding partner of Brillstein-Grey Entertainment, he headed one of the most enviable multitiered and vertically integrated operations in the entertainment universe.

The client list is impressive: Brad Pitt, Gwyneth Paltrow, Jennifer Aniston, Orlando Bloom, Natalie Portman, Adam Sandler, Christian Slater, Courteney Cox, Rob Lowe, and a smorgasbord of others. The shows he got on the air include everything from *Hee Haw* and *The Muppets* to *Saturday Night Live* and *The Sopranos*. *The Muppets*' Jim Henson and *SNL*'s John Belushi and Gilda Radner became legends under Bernie's guidance. They were starving startups when Bernie banked on them. The rest, as they say, is show business history. (After more than thirty years, *Saturday Night Live* creator and executive producer Lorne Michaels remained a client to Bernie's dying day.) "Nobody ever leaves," Bernie said, looking as astounded to say it as I did to hear it. According to a highly reputable source, Michaels said that after Bernie, he would never sign with another manager again, as no one could come even close.

"The words of a man's mouth are as deep waters," King Solomon said, and the words that Bernie's father spoke to him as his mentally ill mother lay struggling for her life in a New York hospital bed bring tears to his eyes to this day. "Do you want to end up a loser like me? Don't end up like me," Moe Brillstein told his son when he had a chance to move to Los Angeles and pursue his own destiny—not a matter of chance, as William Jennings Bryan noted, it is a matter of choice; it is not a thing to be waited for, it is a thing to be achieved. The day Bernie was scheduled to board a plane, he went to see his mother at Doctors' Hospital. All the relatives were there and they let Bernie know just what a disappointment of a son he was: How can you go to California? You've got to stay…how dare you?"

"My father was far from a loser," Bernie said, "but I knew what he meant." Biting down hard on the sentence, Moe got in Bernie's face: "Get out of here." Bernie headed for the airport. "I had a B-24 bag, the kind that pilots used during the war, with tape around it and all my worldly goods in it."

Moe was six months old in 1898 when the Brillsteins fled a little town on the Russia-Poland border called Mizerwicz and came to Harlem. At that time, Harlem had already become a collection of shantytowns and tenements where the brand-new immigrants flocked. Bernie's grandparents and baby Moe were among them.

When he became a success, Bernie offered to send his father to Mizerwicz, to see his birthplace. "I didn't know all that was left were twenty thousand graves," he said somberly. Bernie offered to send Moe to London, Japan, Israel—anywhere he wanted to go. But the answer was always the same: "Nah, I don't want to go there."

When Moe died in 1990, Bernie was going through his father's private belongings when it dawned on him just why his father refused to travel. "My old man was petrified to leave the country because he thought they wouldn't let him come back. I'm not even sure he ever had a passport."

While Moe had a reputation for not wanting to bother anyone with his problems, such was not the case with his mother. "Her *mishegas* affected everyone," Bernie shook his head. Tillie Brillstein lived a lonely life because she rarely got out of bed.

"Occasionally, she'd show up at the dinner table for a meal, but it was like watching a ghost," Bernie recalled. No one knew it at the time, but she suffered from clinical depression. "Her doctors treated her by handing out pills like they were candy—lots of them," Bernie said angrily. "I'd get home and find her conked out on Tuinal or worse. She gradually became a basket case who required constant attention and service from everyone."

Bernie's brother dealt with the family dysfunction by going into the finishing-and-dyeing business, while Bernie sought comfort from food and relied on humor. He also became determined to achieve great success.

In 1955, when he was twenty-four years old, like some other show business greats Bernie got a job in the famed William Morris Agency mail room. "Like every other young guy who worked alongside me, my first thought was, 'How quickly can I get the hell out of here and become a *real* agent?' But unlike the rest of the lot, Bernie didn't wait to be picked form the crop. He worked diligently and sought opportunities and invented and reinvented himself over and over again, and like all great emperors, he crowned himself.

Life is a risk, Bernie understood. Every success comes with some risk attached—often quite a load. "But if you avoid risk," he warned, "you will avoid everything that makes life worth living."

Early on, he also learned about the difference between perception and reality. Bernie's family and grandparents lived with his Uncle Jack Pearl, the famous comedian who was best known for his NBC Radio role as the Baron Munchausen, and his Aunt Winifred Desborough Pearl, a Ziegfeld girl, in their posh nine-room apartment in the swanky El Dorado, at 90th Street and Central Park, until Bernie was nine years old.

When he was eight, everyone gathered at the living room windows to watch as the lights of the 1939 World's Fair were turned on for the first time. "Aunt Winnie hoisted me up by the armpits and held me high so I can also see. She pointed to a dark patch in the distance," Bernie explained. "Suddenly, there was a burst of light brighter than the flash of a thousand cameras at a movie premiere, and the fair was officially open." This was an important early lesson for Bernie: *Life always looks better from the top.*

It would be a while before Bernie got anywhere near the top. "I was the poorest kid in a rich neighborhood," he said. He wasn't sent to tony private schools like the rest of his friends; instead he was shuffled off to public school. Home life presented its own challenges. "Most of the time, my parents didn't get along," he said. "I could always hear them arguing."

Bernie appointed himself the referee and peacekeeper. "I couldn't go to sleep until I made them make up. I'd fix them sandwiches hoping they'd stop battling and start eating." It worked for about a day. As Bernie matured, he realized that his father found it impossible to live with an invalid whose illness he did not understand. "I guess that explains why he slept on the couch in the foyer for twenty years," he said.

"Now you see why my family was the perfect basic training for a life in show business," he said, as if making a profound revelation. "In one way or another, for more than fifty years, I've continued to referee, to wait on the needy, to make sandwiches for peace, and to pull guard duty—they call it being a personal manager."

The hard way, he also grasped the concept of dignity—or lack of it. Bernie said that for most of his childhood, he did not know that Uncle Jack paid for the apartment. "I found out when he started giving me mysterious envelopes for my father. I looked inside and discovered cash. It destroyed me." A trace of pain still crossed his face. "Later, my father told me that he'd been my uncle's de facto manager—without getting a full manager's cut. My dad already had a job, so what he did for the family was expected and considered part-time. In exchange, my uncle paid some of the bills." Bernie explained that his father was never bitter, but later told him that he thought he'd been shortchanged. "He gave me a little money, but never ten percent," Moe said to Bernie. "It was a lesson I didn't forget." While undermining people's dignity is a classic expression of passive-aggressive pathology, it is also "negative, manipulative, cowardly, and pathetic." He added, "It is also common among useless managers and bosses all throughout the industry."

When the Pearls couldn't handle the Brillsteins any longer, the Brillsteins moved to a smaller apartment on the third floor. There, they inherited Uncle Benny, an alcoholic who left their uptown building every morning, with a sack lunch, for his job at the post office.

"My family may have been neurotic," Bernie said, "but they gave me much more than simply an education in dealing with head cases. Thanks to my uncle and father, I experienced New York's two distinct show business cultures—the East Side and the West Side." Bernie learned to feel at home in the Stork Club and the Carnegie Deli, and could get a table at both. "By the time I went to New York University," Bernie added, "I knew the language of the swells and the streets. I could talk to anyone."

After college in 1953, Bernie was drafted into the army. "The only way I'd go," he said. "I had never been far from New York, so I decided to make it a test to see if I could get along in an environment over which I had no control. I was a Jew from New York in a world with few Jews, and not that many people from New York, either." After basic training, Bernie was posted in England. "I kept from doing any real work by doing what came naturally—I produced shows. I'd seen a transvestite revue in college," he explained, "in which people from the audience were called onstage to dance in a number called "Balling the Jack." So I stole it. Only I made sure officers were summoned to dance with guys in drag." Very pleased with himself, Bernie mused, "It was hilarious—and it kept me busy."

Upon his return in 1955, Bernie concluded that he needed a real job. He was restless. "I knew that the world was a bigger place than the garment center and the Millinery Center Synagogue fund-raising shows," he said. After a brief stint as a television station commercial salesman in Hartford, Connecticut, on behalf of *Lassie*, Bernie had to consider different career options. After a game of softball in Central Park with his friend and NYU fraternity brother, Billy Rubin, an opportunity presented itself. "You know, Bernie, you'd make a helluva agent," Billy said, and he set up a meeting with Lou Weiss at the William Morris Agency.

"It seemed like a good idea," Bernie said. "Show business was in my blood. I knew the rhythms, the politics, the people. In fact, Billy's suggestion made so much sense that to this day I don't know why I didn't think of it first."

Monday, June 5, 1955, wearing the only suit he owned, Bernie got on a city bus and went to work in the William Morris mail room for $38 a week—$32.81 after taxes. "I started at William Morris with four goals in mind: make some steady money, have the one performer everyone wanted, get the phone calls instead of having to make them, and know everyone when I walked into a restaurant and have them know me." But first, Bernie had to get promoted out of the mail room. Part of the plan included some sneaky-peeky spying.

"On my first trip outside the office, I delivered a $25,000 check to Red Buttons at 50 Sutton Place South. I knew what was in the envelope because, like any ambitious guy with a head on his shoulders, I opened all the interesting-looking letters and packages before handing them over." Bernie added, "Everyone did it because information is king. We'd go into the men's room, run the water hot as possible and wait for the steam to do the rest, read and carefully reseal." This way, Bernie found client lists, contracts, personal correspondence, as well as checks. "I never worried about being caught, because another guy from the mail room was often at the next sink doing the same thing."

Schlepping around New York carrying kinescopes and heavy film cans was no holiday for a heavy-set guy, and Bernie would have rather stayed at the office. "In order to steam envelopes, read memos, plot and plan, and learn the business," he said, "I had to be *in the building.*" That's the big lesson: *put yourself where the action is.* "It helps if you love the action," Bernie said. "If not, you're in the wrong business."

Everyone in the mail room had the same objective: get the hell out as quickly as possible and become a real agent. "We competed against each other like a school of baby sharks," Bernie said. But only a few would grow up to be, well, big sharks.

"As long as I stayed in the mail room I couldn't earn anyone's respect," he went on to say. "I'd just be another office boy who jumped when someone said, 'Go get me lunch.'" Bernie said he always believed that people who *want* the jobs *get* the jobs. "They're never content to sit and wait to be noticed." He added, "Any schmuck can do that, and lots of schmucks have."

But "I knew how to be discovered." Bernie explained, "Kiss ass—but not the big executives. I didn't want to reach too far, too soon."

No one ever gained an advantage by imitation, and soon enough, Bernie got out of the mail room by finding a weak link in the company, someone whose personality and job performance created an opportunity. "I could have tried to be an agent's secretary, but what for?" He explained, "When you're on a toll bridge, you try and pick the line that moves the quickest. Some people wait for the best job. Some people wait for the middle job. I didn't care—I wanted *anything!* I thought, 'Just get me out of here, because no one's gonna know I have any talent *until* I get out of here.'"

The way out was the road least traveled. Jerry Collins was the head of publicity. He was middle-aged, rumpled-looking, and always had a cigarette dangling out of his mouth. Bernie did Jerry favors until one day, he acted like he was giving Bernie the keys to the executive bathroom. "You seem bright," he said. "How would you like to work with me?" The reality of the matter: his assistant quit.

Everyone in the mail room knew it was grunt work and the chorus sang: "Don't take the job!" Bernie did otherwise. "I knew three things," he said. "One, the publicity office was opposite Nat Kalcheim's office [head of the personal appearance office and the most respected man at the agency], and proximity is priceless. Two, in publicity you worked with *everyone* in the company; thus, the job provided maximum exposure to agents, clients, and others who could help me take the next step up. And three, I'd be *out of the mail room!*"

He also knew that Nat Kalcheim, like too many others in the organization, as he would later discover, lacked imagination and creativity. At the end of the day, this is largely due to fear—the fear of taking a risk; the fear of being wrong; the fear of being held accountable. While executives like to be seen as courageous risk-takers, most of them are as timid as a church mouse when it comes to doing anything different than their peers in the industry. In a broad sense, "That's why most manage mediocre businesses with mediocre success and mediocre products—whether you're considering a film actor or a new car." Perhaps imitation feels safe because you never stand out enough to attract criticism. "Sadly," Bernie added, "your results will never stand out, either."

A culture and an environment that does not foster risk-taking is the biggest impediment to innovation. "We have focus groups," Bernie explained, "consultants, experts in image, marketing, you name it…but at the end of the day, it doesn't cut it in the innovation stakes because they don't foster risk-taking." The successful people who operate on intuitive instinct understand that you cannot be innovative and risk-averse simultaneously. "Change and risk are joined at the hip," Bernie reminds us. In fact, the more innovative the change, the greater is the risk.

"Many people get *risk* all wrong," Bernie said, "because they focus entirely on the *risk of being wrong*." But what about the *risk* of being right? Maybe even more right than you ever dreamed…. "Much of the success in the real world has to do with acting on your instinct, not on design," Bernie noted. After all, if there was a formula, everyone would be successful. Of course, you will get it wrong regardless. But, "the real crime in lack of success is stagnation and a dull mind, not making honest mistakes." What's the bottom line? "Think for yourself," Bernie said. "Life changes, circumstances change, public taste and opinion changes. What worked so well yesterday can be a liability today and a disaster tomorrow."

Bernie belabors the point that those who apply only tried-and-true business practices will never break out of mediocrity, will never become distinguished. "You cannot ignore the reality that change is constant.... The first solid step into the future is always to let go of the past."

In addition to keen observation, shrewd imagination, and risk-taking, Bernie further relied on target-oriented visualization in order to create the desired realities in his life. "This probably sounds terrible," he now says, "but it's the truth: throughout my career I always imagined the guy I worked for getting fired and me taking his job." He added, " I could always see myself moving up."

"Without a vision, the people perish," King Solomon stated. Call it what you will, so many ordinary people who have achieved extraordinary things use the power of creative visualization—knowingly or subconsciously—to turn their dreams into reality. They know how to identify what they want in life and then use the power of their imagination to create it. In other words, if you can see a picture of what you want in your mind's eye, by holding this image as often as possible, in time, you will see the thing imagined appear in your life. Proponents of the law of attraction say that when you understand that everything is energy—the entire universe and everything in it—it is easier to understand the process of creative visualization.

"You reap what you sow" or "what you give is what you get" means that your habitual thinking creates your reality. "Everything starts as an idea," Bernie reminds us. "If you believe in something, it will manifest."

It worked. When Jerry Collins got canned, Bernie took over.

"Here's what I learned from him," Bernie said, "absolutely nothing." It was the firm's lowest-paying job. "My pay in publicity never topped $75."

When opportunity knocks you'd better be ready to answer, Bernie believes, whether or not you're supposed to. One day Ed Bondy, an agent in the legit department, ran into publicity to see Bernie. He said, "Molly Picon is leaving *Milk and Honey*"—a Broadway show about Israel—"and none of us know any Yiddish actresses who can take her place. You do because of your Uncle Jack."

Bernie thought for a moment and said the only other Yiddish actress he knew was Jenny Goldstein. "Great," said Ed and left to call the producers. He returned in time and breathlessly said, "They're thrilled. They'll buy Jenny Goldstein and give her $500 a week."

"I reminded him that she was a star. I said, 'She won't work for $500. Get her $750 a week.'" He called the producers again and got the $750. Then he called Jenny Goldstein only to discover that Jenny Goldstein had been dead for four years.

"Now that's classic agenting," Bernie boasted of his first big deal. "I got a dead person a $250 raise. I knew I was in the right business."

Bernie got out of publicity the same way he got out of the mail room. "I looked for a weak link." He found it in the commercial department. Lee Karsian was his boss, but not for long. When he got fired—visualization again—Bernie took his place. "Putting clients in commercials wasn't the same as booking talent into nightclubs or on TV, but since it was a new department and outside of the mainstream, I felt like I had my own little business inside William Morris—I decided to make the best of it."

Bernie was consistently practical, but he was idealistic, too. "Many people believe that show business—perhaps no different than any other competitive business—is a nasty, tough, and brutish existence," he said. "It's dog-eat-dog and you better accept that. If you cannot, you must step aside and let others take over who aren't queasy." Idealism is totally out of fashion. It appears that it is necessary for anyone who wishes to succeed to be hard, aggressive, and unburdened by scruples. "So is the belief that mankind is capable of freeing itself from the issues caused by ignorance, greed, poverty, and tyranny," Bernie commented.

The new job had many rewards, and Bernie was a trailblazer in the celebrity endorsement industry as television arrived on the scene in the '50s. One day in 1960, Burr Tillstrom, the puppeteer and creator of the TV show *Kukla, Fran and Ollie*, called. "I'd just gotten his three hand-operated stars a TV commercial," Bernie recalled, "so he asked me to do him a favor and meet with a friend." Tillstrom said the friend needed an agent.

"Christ, Burr," Bernie told him. "Maybe I can get him a commercial, but beyond that, what do I know about puppets?"

"You'll like him," Tillstrom assured Bernie. "He's funny. See him." Bernie had no desire to see him, but he threw in the towel.

When the guy showed up, "I couldn't believe my eyes," Bernie recalled. "In walked this guy who looked like a cross between Abraham Lincoln and Jesus—six-three in a hippie arts-and-crafts leather suit. He wore a beard—which I later discovered was to cover his acne scars. He was so gentle and unpretentious that he never spoke above a whisper. He'd brought a big box of puppets. When he put them on his hands, it was magic."

His name was Jim Henson. "We were together thirty years, until he died," Bernie said. "I did it on instinct. There was nothing logical about it.

"Making out once is luck. Twice is coincidence. Do it three times or more," he said, "and maybe you know something. If you follow up enough of your hunches, maybe one day people may call you a genius," Bernie mused coyly. "To me it's the continuity of luck that's interesting," he said. "Instinct is not something you can learn. Having and using instinct separates the people who should be in the business from those who often are." Is selective instinct this great asset? "Feeling the fear, pain, and hope of the other person," he said, "that's my greatest asset."

Some people think instinct means understanding why a performer or a show or a film is a hit today. "Wrong," Bernie flat-out stated. "It means you can see someone who's not yet hot and feel the potential for greatness." Bernie explained that instinct also means that you know the difference between hot and good; between style and substance. "They're *not* the same," he insists. "These days we have too much hot—performers who are flavors of the week for maybe a day and a half, and then they're gone. I think the public resents the over-hyping."

It's much easier to sell a hype than it is the reality. Myths can still become self-fulfilling prophecies because they haven't failed yet. Hollywood is full of myths that people keep buying "because everyone wants to be known as the discoverer," Bernie stated. "Everyone wants to say, 'I found…'"

It is great to be hot. "You get three jobs from it," Bernie said. "You're not judged by your talent and your long-term prospects. You're just the thing that will make someone money *now*. Anyone can get hot: agents, managers, lawyers, writers, and a model who will swim topless at a horny director's house. I've seen hot," Bernie explained. "It burns bright, but lasts only a moment."

Bernie Brillstein turns hot into good or just finds good and builds lifelong careers. "The people we represent have careers, which is why we represent them," he said. Although anyone can trip over talent, it doesn't mean they can stay with the talent, guide the talent in the right direction, or keep them successful. But if your client has a career, Bernie said, only then are you a successful manager. A good analogy for the whole process is the difference between an artist like Renoir and someone using a paint-by-the numbers kit. One does it faster and it doesn't require much ability, but whose work would you prefer to own?

After years of diligent and innovative efforts under the ownership of others, Bernie preferred to own himself. "One reason I started the Brillstein Company in 1968 is that I never wanted to ask myself, 'So now what?'" He added, "My greatest fear has always been to be [at a certain] age and have to go looking for a job."

When Bernie was a kid, he saw *Death of a Salesman* on Broadway, "and it scared the life out of me," he said. Willy Loman is loyal to the firm for forty-odd years and then they just dump him. "Every working man's nightmare must be that he's replaceable." Bernie warned, "That's why you go into business for yourself—better to be an owner than to depend on someone else to have your best interest at heart."

The Brillstein Company consisted of Bernie, his then wife, Laura, Sandy Wenrick, and a couple of secretaries. "Sandy probably knows more about how show business works than anyone not currently at a movie studio or TV network," Bernie praised his colleague. "He's the consummate inside man who can execute a deal. That lets me handle the people and the strategy. With him as my second in command," Bernie added, "we quickly developed a working relationship that in twenty-three years has come to resemble an old married couple."

Bernie Brillstein is a noted gambler, and he placed his bet in 1985 on a twenty-six-year-old, long-haired, chubby-cheeked, bright and ambitious guy named Brad Grey. "[There was] something about him," Bernie mused, "the look of resolve in his eyes, the way he cut through the chronic [nonsense] and got to the point, made me feel like he got it: the truth about show business and the way things really work. Even though we had different styles of doing business, from day one, as the years went by, we were a great team."

In 1989, Bernie made Brad Grey his partner. In 1992, Bernie cofounded Brillstein-Grey Entertainment, simply *the* most successful management-production company of the '90s and beyond. In 1999, Bernie made Brad his boss when he sold him his half of the company. A year ago, Sumner Redstone made Brad Grey the chairman of Paramount. Hence, it is evident that Bernie not only recognized the best in entertainment talent, but the best in the entertainment business.

What did Bernie Brillstein learn on the way to coronation? That in business, reputation is worth hard cash. He put much of it in a book called *The Little Stuff Matters: 50 Rules from 50 Years of Trying to Make a Living*. During our conversations, he reiterated some of it and shared much more about what really makes him tick.

First of all, "My wink is binding," he said. At the beginning, it was stated that no client ever left. Well, what's even more incredible in this day and age is that no client ever had a contract with Bernie. "A contract is something you break," he said. It wasn't a conscious choice initially. At first, Bernie simply found contracts to be "boring and too fat for me to read." Then he wondered, "If you're in business with someone for two or three years, why would you give them another contract?" Eventually he realized, "You know they're going to screw you or not screw you after a short while, so why bother with a contract?" He made his point: "In all of my years—oh [man], fifty-four years already—no one has beat me out of a penny."

What does he attribute this to? "That they have no contracts." I raised an eyebrow. "I know this sounds insane," he said, "but people are mostly moral. They also know that you can bad-mouth them and that's bad for business. They also know they can leave any time they want…but after ten years, it's like a marriage—you get to the point it's not worth leaving unless you do something *really* wrong."

In the wicked world of Hollywood, Bernie has earned a virtually unprecedented reputation of never screwing anyone. "And I won't do it," he said adamantly. "I just turned seventy-six and no one's gonna kill me."

With a fair dose of modesty, he explained that "you just go on and you work every day. And if you do well, you can work until you're a hundred if your senses are all there. People want to work with you because they know you're creative and because they don't have to worry about the deal." He thought for a moment and added, "People stay up all night sweating about the deal...but I want to see first just what we have, and only when I can help you, the lawyer will make the deal." Less modestly, after more than half a century in the business, he offered a penetrating glimpse into the obvious. "I don't think that anyone has the brain that I have."

It all begins at home. "Bring your manners from home to work," Bernie said. "I was brought up by a moralistic father who walked on the edge of morals—both ways. And, thanks to my Aunt Winnie, I was brought up with great manners. As you know, my mother wasn't well. But I watched my father, and he was so good with people and they loved him." What Bernie learned to appreciate was the value of every place and experience. "I liked the East and the West," he said, literally and metaphorically. "And that's what we do here...if you bring your manners and your class and your dignity to show business, which is known for not having manners, dignity, or class—you will do well."

Bring your knowledge along as well. "I know everything about the history of show business in the world," he said as a matter of fact. "And if you read all those books and you don't know what to do, you're an idiot." Bernie finds fault with the fact that young people today don't read those books. They read the *Wall Street Journal* instead. "Remember," he stated, "you're going to be pounding on the pavement and searching out opportunity, but you only need one person—ONE—to have the best life in the world." He thought for a moment and said, "Look, I'm not saying I knew Jim Henson was a genius when I met him. But I knew he made me laugh. When I took on Jim, people in New York laughed at me." Back to instinct: "When people walk into my office, within two seconds I know whether I like them or not; you have to *feel* something."

What Bernie feels is worth hundreds of millions at the bank. But unlike a ball-busting, fear-mongering and *Art of War* worshipping, gone-into oblivion ("It's amazing how I managed to survive without him!") Mike Ovitz, for example, Bernie Brillstein is a God-fearing gentle giant. It's about the long game. He's among the few who comprehend that greed and ego are bad for business. "I'm driven by God," he said with total conviction and no apologies. "Now, I'm not one of those people who thinks and acts like it's all about God, but I do believe that there's a guy out there with a beard who looks a lot like me and he has a little book with X and Y columns." Bernie explained, "If you tip a cab driver five bucks extra, you get a little check mark; if you stiff a cab driver, that's an X. I believe if you're rude to people, that goes on one side, and if you're good, that goes on the other."

It may be karma, or "you reap what you sow" simply explained; nevertheless, "It's been my motivation my whole life," he said. "Do you know how I know it's real?" he asked. "It's when I was broke," he confessed. "I said a prayer to myself. I owed seventy grand and I didn't have a nickel. I prayed, 'God, if you get me even, I will tip everyone for the rest of my life. I will give people money. I will do anything you want—just get me even.'"

God said to Abraham, "I will bless you that you may *be* a blessing." And Bernie was blessed. "He got me even," Bernie said, still grateful. "You think you get away with anything? You get away with *nothing*." He continued the dialogue, "Now am I nuts? Maybe." Bernie explained, "I haven't been to a synagogue in thirty years. It's not about religion, it's about faith. Man invented religion, but God is real. God is the boss of bosses. He's the good Tony Soprano—the family deserves respect because he put us all here." After a pause, he declared, "I will always be on the right side of everything. I wouldn't trust many other people to do that, but I trust myself."

He drifted into a time long gone, laser-beamed into my eyes, and said, "You know, my father was so basic…but I followed his path with the one line he said to me at the hospital as my mother lay dying. 'Get the hell out of here.'" After what appeared to be the longest silence, he uttered, "And that was it, it's the truth. The truth makes you cry, you know?"

It was a particularly divine March afternoon as I walked over to Bernie's office from the Peninsula Hotel. Bernie came for the final interview. The cast was removed from his leg and with the help of Darko, his trusty personal trainer, he had shed twenty pounds. "I look good, don't I?" He beamed mischievously. Within minutes he turned pensive. "Today marks twenty-five years," he said and looked at his watch, "to the hour, that I got a call about John Belushi," his voice trailed off. Carefully, in grave detail and tear-filled eyes, he recounted the events of the tragic day, of his solitary plane ride with the body back to Belushi's home. "We couldn't save him," he said, still devastated. How are you marking the occasion? I asked. "I talk to God…"

At the end of the day, he summed it all up: "All the grief I've had; all the horrors I've experienced; all the success that went beyond the moon and reached the stars. And you know what? It comes down to a dog and a wife—someone to love and who loves you, and thank God I know *that's the truth!*"

“Without the understanding that people can change their circumstances and transform their lives, we wouldn’t have survived the Ice Age, let alone the Atomic Age.”

CONCLUSION

THERE ARE THOSE WHO claim that individual effort, disciplined awareness, and strong values play no—repeat, *no*—role in success. These social scientists see humans as agglomerations of humanity, not individuals with unique souls. They track humans in their collective endeavors, categorizing them accordingly, analyzing what they have in common—and presto, a theory is born. To wit: it's not what you know or do or believe that matters. Not at all. The only important determinants to success are your family position, your birthplace, and even your birth date. If you were born before, or after, key years in the development of the modern American economy, you cannot possibly participate in the computer and software boom that has characterized its greatest growth. You cannot possibly know the right people, or have the right connections, or obtain the proper knowledge to really succeed in this world.

How then do we explain the simple fact that many people of ordinary backgrounds, even backgrounds of great deprivation, have risen, through their own efforts, to commanding heights of success? How do we explain the story of Dr. Steven Hoefflin, who started out with a paper route and became one of the world's foremost plastic surgeons? Or the story of John Paul DeJoria, who was sleeping in his car before he became a fabulously wealthy entrepreneur and philanthropist?

Over and over, throughout history, it is possible to find a different explanation for success. It is obviously not automatic that someone born into wealth and privilege will succeed in life. There are too many examples of this to list here. By the same token, the examples cited in this book prove that the extraordinary efforts and insights of a single gifted, driven person can create that which no charmed childhood can.

So just what is success? We have seen many answers to this question in this book. Taken together, it is possible to see that one thing common to everyone in this book is the ability to adapt to adversity, learn from mistakes, and try again. And again. This is not a quality handed to special people at the moment of their birth. This is not a quality exclusive to certain classes, ethnic groups, or religions. It is innate in all humans. We are the only creatures who think, reason, and project our thinking onto the world in complex ways. It would seem unfair to reduce us to the coincidences of birth, class, and geography. To do that takes everything that drives people to achieve and reduces it to a mere set of economic principles. This might work for social scientists and Marxists, but does it really explain the human drive to succeed?

People are infinitely adaptable. We have seen a transformation of humanity, from being one among many species competing for dominance to being the dominant species on the planet. We have conquered the earth, the air, the sea, and space. We have cracked the genetic code and peered into the farthest reaches of our universe. Yet, we still struggle. We still adapt to new discoveries and ideas and events. We still ask the ancient questions: What are we doing here? What is the meaning of life?

We seek answers to things that we didn't even dream about not so long ago, and we seek ways of understanding our world and our destinies by challenging that which has gone before. This process of renewal and reaffirmation has led to some of our greatest triumphs—and they have not been determined by a few privileged members of very privileged times and classes and places.

The triumph of the human race has been a story of many shocks absorbed, many disasters overcome, many dreams realized. As history has progressed and the world has gotten smaller, more people have been included in the idea of individual achievement, individual development, and self-realization. The more people have awakened to their own potential and been empowered to achieve it, the more successfully societies have fought the problems facing them.

In other words, progress has been achieved by the individual who strives to leave an imprint on the world. It is not privilege that has made it possible for the individual to succeed; it is the will to adapt, learn, and overcome. It is not possible to read the stories of the amazing individuals in this book without realizing that the human capacity to conquer adversity is infinite.

There is literally no limit to what a determined person can achieve. What gave these people their determination? In some cases they had to overcome circumstances bad enough to make them consider quitting altogether. Indeed, people faced with much less calamity have dropped out of the struggle, daunted beyond their ability to respond.

What kept the people in this book going? What fueled them? It's different for each, but they all share an unwillingness to submit to anyone else's definition of failure. How many people hear "no" and, nodding to themselves, accept it as a judgment on them and all their work? How many people are merely looking for an excuse to quit trying? How many will accept the judgment of others as gospel and abandon themselves as a result? Too many.

This book seeks to send a simple message, yet one that needs to be reaffirmed every generation: Don't ever give up. Ever. Whatever fuels your determination, hang on to it, nurture it, and use it. This may mean faith in God, a desire to answer critics, or the need to express yourself through a form of art, business, intellectual pursuits, humanitarian efforts, or the calm awareness of your own worth. Whatever it is, consider how much bleaker the world would be without the determination of a few people to make it better. Consider how much poorer we would all be if everyone took every "no" seriously. And consider what was accomplished by people who were unwilling to accept "no" for an answer.

We can see this phenomenon in religious doctrine. Faith, that mysterious belief in a divine order, is universally the text, subtext, and context of all religion. Without a willingness to believe that the universe is more than human senses can perceive, and that there seem to be patterns of human behavior that correspond to the best ideals of this faith, then people will collapse into fear, idolatry, and anarchy. Faith, then, has been an important engine of human endeavor. It has also been a guide, a shield, and an organizing principle for millennia. To ignore it is to ignore one of the most enduring human institutions, one that explains us as much as any social science. Faith has moved mountains, crossed oceans, and conquered space. Is it really possible that it had nothing to do with the advancement of the world, that the work of a few people, born at the right place at the right time, are responsible for all progress? I don't think so.

The theme of this book has been transformation. The idea that people can change their circumstances, have a positive impact on their own lives, and overcome the problems they face is central to the human spirit. Without this adaptability we would not have survived the Ice Age, much less the Atomic Age. Survival of the species may no longer be at stake, but individual survival still is. And one of the keys to survival is the ability to transform.

Success can be measured in a number of ways, but certain elements of it are universal: the ability to raise a family in peace and security, the certainty that your efforts today will lead to greater prosperity tomorrow, and the knowledge that what you have done in your life will benefit the generations that will follow you. To accomplish these things, we need more than a mere plan or single philosophy. We must have faith—faith that we are on the right track, that we have learned the right lessons, and that we have the right tools to overcome any unforeseen developments.

Where does faith come from? There are many answers, but one is that faith comes from knowledge of what it has accomplished in the past. If you know how faith has helped you in your own life, then what will a real understanding of the ways faith has helped millions of humans in thousands of cultures do? Such an understanding should provide you with the means to confront those challenges that you will inevitably face. Properly perceived, it should provide you with an understanding of your own strength.

Remember that you are the inheritor of generations of strugglers. You are the beneficiary of the experiments, the sacrifices, and the striving of all your ancestors. They have bequeathed to you, and to all of us, a message that we need to relearn in every generation. The ghosts of our past have gathered in their millions to remind us that nothing worth doing was ever accomplished easily, that no one can escape the demands of life, and that we are all part of this enterprise. The catastrophes we have overcome should empower us to marshal our incredible resources to tackle the problems we face every day. We all have amazing resources at our disposal, many of which we aren't even aware of. Sometimes the only thing that makes us aware is a disaster. But once we are mobilized to seize control of our lives, the process gets easier. We realize that we have the strength, the resilience, and the will to transform our circumstances and destinies. This may be the most precious realization of all and the greatest gift from our past—not what pitfalls await us, but how nature has equipped us to overcome. We are the inheritors of a rich and tumultuous past. It has provided us with example after example of what can be achieved by the proper cultivation and mobilization of the human spirit.

Faith, perseverance, knowledge, wisdom, awareness, forgiveness, and love are all part of our collective inheritance. Now that you have seen how these qualities have helped some individuals have extraordinary lives, you can make the transformations that you need in yours. You have all the tools you need. All you have to do is put them to good use.

ACKNOWLEDGMENTS

I WISH TO THANK ALL the exceptional people who have been a part of my life journey and ongoing life transformation; those who have taken me to higher ground as well as the oppressors, for there are no enemies, only teachers.

I am grateful beyond measure to Dwight D. Opperman for showing me, by example, just what an extraordinary human being is. If I achieve a mere fraction of the integrity, humility, and humanity that he possesses, my life will be complete.

If you don't have a Michael Viner in your life, I strongly suggest you get one. A Viner is a person who will go to the front lines for you but will simultaneously aim the cannon at you—and shoot—if it means bringing the best out of you. This makes for the best publisher and friend I could hope for—I think.

I thank Larry King for his numerous kindnesses on a daily basis. To know him is to understand why he truly is King.

I thank the sea of people who have been a part of this book in one form or other since its incarnation. They have all left an indelible impression on me, especially James Nederlander, Cindy Adams, Mark Burnett, and the late Bernie Brillstein. I am grateful to Barbara Guggenheim for her endless wit and wisdom.

I am most appreciative of the twelve who moved the mountain and shared their extraordinary stories with me, often under challenging circumstances. They include John Paul DeJoria, right after he returned from his heartwrenching journey through South Africa; Paula White, who was mourning the death of her daughter; Jacqueline Jakes, who is engaged in a massive effort to help AIDS children with her brother, Bishop T. D. Jakes; David Foster, right after his studio burned down; Justice Clarence Thomas, who was up at the crack of dawn in Florence, Italy, beating sense into me; Dr. Patch Adams, who flew from Russia to spend Halloween with me at the Peninsula in Beverly Hills, where he told me stories of children dying in his arms; José Eber, whose talent and strength of character rises above all the greedy and brutal acts inflicted upon him; Judge Sol Wachtler, who swallowed his pride and opened his heart and soul during dreary New York nights; Dr. Steven Hoefflin, who spent many hours on the phone and behind his computer in Mexico, where he was working with mentally challenged children; Paul Anka, who made it for a day from his European tour; and Robert Evans, who opened up his entire world to make sure that I got exactly what I wanted.

To all of you, Amen.

A special thanks to all the talented and hardworking people at Phoenix Books, Inc.; Dove Books, Inc.; my great editor, C. M. Talley; and Newman Communications, Inc. for your considerable efforts and dedication.

As always, thank you to the best brother a girl ever had—George Stankovich.

Julie Chrystyn